Digital Cosmos

Digital Cosmos

Matthew Petchinsky

publisher logo

Digital Cosmos: The Astrological Digimon Compendium
By: Matthew Petchinsky

Introduction
Welcome to the Digital Cosmos
Overview of the Book's Purpose

Welcome to "Digital Cosmos: The Astrological Digimon Compendium," a unique journey that explores the fascinating intersection of Digimon, astrology, and celestial events. This book is designed to offer readers an enriching experience by blending the digital adventures of Digimon with the timeless wisdom of astrology. Whether you are a seasoned fan of Digimon, a devoted follower of astrology, or someone who is curious about both realms, this compendium aims to provide a fresh perspective on how these two worlds can interconnect in meaningful and insightful ways.

The primary purpose of this book is to bridge the gap between the digital and celestial, illustrating how the characters and stories within the Digimon universe align with the astrological signs, planets, and various celestial events that influence our lives. By delving into this compendium, you will gain a deeper understanding of how the personalities and journeys of your favorite Digimon reflect astrological principles, as well as how celestial phenomena can shape their narratives.

Explanation of Integration of Digimon and Astrology Concepts

At first glance, the digital world of Digimon and the ancient art of astrology might seem worlds apart. However, upon closer examination, they share remarkable similarities in themes, archetypes, and the idea of personal growth and transformation. This book will guide you through the process of integrating these concepts in a way that is both accessible and enlightening.

Each chapter will focus on different aspects of astrology – including the twelve zodiac signs, the nine planets, celestial bodies like the moon and the sun, moon phases, and significant celestial events such as eclipses and planetary alignments. Alongside these astrological elements, we will introduce corresponding Digimon characters and storylines that embody the essence of these cosmic forces. Through this synthesis, you will see how Digimon can personify the traits and energies associated with each astrological component, making the abstract concepts of astrology more tangible and relatable.

For instance, you will discover how the bold and adventurous spirit of Agumon resonates with the fiery energy of Aries, or how the deep, emotional nature of Gabumon mirrors the intuitive and sensitive qualities of Cancer. By linking Digimon to specific zodiac signs and celestial events, we will unveil a new layer of understanding and appreciation for both Digimon and astrology.

Brief Introduction to Digimon and Basic Astrology Concepts

Before we dive into the intricate connections between Digimon and astrology, it is essential to have a basic understanding of both worlds.

Digimon:

Digimon, short for Digital Monsters, is a multimedia franchise that includes anime, manga, video games, toys, and more. The core concept revolves around digital creatures that inhabit a parallel "Digital World" and can evolve into more powerful forms through a process called "Digivolution." Digimon are partnered with human characters, typically children, who embark on adventures to protect both the Digital World and the real world from various threats. Each Digimon has unique abilities, attributes, and personalities that contribute to their roles in the overarching narrative.

Astrology:

Astrology is an ancient practice that studies the movements and relative positions of celestial bodies to gain insights into human affairs and natural phenomena. Central to astrology are the twelve zodiac signs, each representing different personality traits and life paths. The positions and movements of planets, the moon, and the sun at the time of a person's birth are believed to influence their character and destiny. Additionally, celestial events such as eclipses, retrogrades, and planetary alignments are thought to have significant effects on both individual lives and the collective consciousness.

In this compendium, we will explore how the traits and archetypes of Digimon characters align with the characteristics of zodiac signs, planets, and celestial events. By doing so, we aim to offer a unique lens through which you can appreciate the depth and richness of both Digimon and astrology.

Join us as we embark on this cosmic journey through the Digital Cosmos, where the stars and the digital world converge in a tapestry of adventure, discovery, and transformation.

Part 1: The Planets and Their Digital Guardians

Chapter 1: The Sun: Agumon's Radiant Leadership
Characteristics of the Sun in Astrology

The Sun is the center of our solar system and the most powerful celestial body in astrology. It represents the core of our being, our identity, and our ego. The Sun symbolizes our life force, vitality, and the essence of who we are at our most fundamental level. It is associated with leadership, self-expression, creativity, and the ability to shine brightly in the world. In the zodiac, the Sun governs the sign of Leo, which is characterized by its warmth, confidence, and natural inclination to lead.

Key characteristics of the Sun in astrology include:

- **Vitality and Energy**: The Sun is a source of life and energy, symbolizing our physical and spiritual vitality.
- **Identity and Ego**: It represents our sense of self, our ego, and our conscious mind.
- **Creativity and Self-Expression**: The Sun encourages us to express ourselves creatively and to shine in our unique way.
- **Leadership and Authority**: The Sun embodies qualities of leadership, authority, and the ability to inspire and guide others.
- **Confidence and Ambition**: It instills a sense of confidence, ambition, and the drive to achieve our goals.
- **Warmth and Generosity**: The Sun's warmth reflects qualities of generosity, kindness, and a nurturing spirit.

Agumon's Attributes as a Digimon Leader

Agumon is one of the most iconic Digimon, known for his bravery, strength, and unwavering loyalty. As the partner Digimon of Tai Kamiya, the leader of the DigiDestined, Agumon plays a crucial role in their adventures, often taking on the mantle of leadership and guiding his friends through challenging situations. Agumon's attributes as a leader are closely aligned with the qualities of the Sun, making him a perfect embodiment of solar energy.

Key attributes of Agumon as a Digimon leader include:

- **Courage and Bravery**: Agumon is fearless in the face of danger, always ready to protect his friends and fight for what is right.
- **Loyalty and Devotion**: He is deeply loyal to Tai and the other DigiDestined, showing unwavering support and dedication.
- **Strength and Resilience**: Agumon possesses immense physical strength and resilience, capable of evolving into more powerful forms like Greymon and WarGreymon to overcome formidable foes.
- **Inspiration and Guidance**: As a leader, Agumon inspires his fellow Digimon and human partners, often taking charge in critical moments and guiding them to victory.
- **Optimism and Positivity**: Agumon maintains a positive attitude even in difficult times, radiating optimism and hope.
- **Protectiveness and Nurturing**: He has a nurturing side, often looking out for the younger or weaker Digimon and ensuring their safety.

How Agumon Embodies the Sun's Energy and Influences

Agumon's character and actions throughout the Digimon series vividly illustrate the Sun's energy and influences. His journey from a small, curious Digimon to a powerful and respected leader mirrors the Sun's role in astrology – a source of life, growth, and inspiration.

1. **Vitality and Energy**: Agumon's boundless energy and enthusiasm are reminiscent of the Sun's vitality. He is always ready to leap into action, displaying a tireless spirit that motivates those around him. Whether it's leading a charge against a menacing en-

emy or exploring new territories in the Digital World, Agumon's energy is infectious, inspiring his friends to keep moving forward.

2. **Identity and Ego**: The Sun's influence on identity and ego is evident in Agumon's strong sense of self. He is confident in his abilities and aware of his role within the DigiDestined team. Agumon's evolution into Greymon and ultimately WarGreymon symbolizes the growth and development of his identity, reflecting the Sun's power to illuminate our true potential.

3. **Creativity and Self-Expression**: Agumon's various Digivolutions showcase his creativity and adaptability. Each transformation, from Agumon to Greymon, MetalGreymon, and WarGreymon, represents a new form of self-expression and strength. These evolutions highlight Agumon's ability to harness the Sun's creative energy, transforming challenges into opportunities for growth and triumph.

4. **Leadership and Authority**: As a natural leader, Agumon exemplifies the Sun's qualities of leadership and authority. He often takes charge in critical situations, providing direction and motivation to his team. Agumon's leadership is not just about strength; it's about his ability to inspire confidence and trust, much like the Sun's role in providing guidance and illumination.

5. **Confidence and Ambition**: Agumon's confidence is unwavering, even in the face of seemingly insurmountable odds. His ambition to protect his friends and defeat their enemies drives him to continually evolve and improve. This relentless pursuit of excellence embodies the Sun's ambitious nature, pushing Agumon to achieve his highest potential.

6. **Warmth and Generosity**: Agumon's warmth and generosity shine through in his interactions with others. He is always willing to lend a helping hand, offer words of encouragement, and support his friends in their times of need. This nurturing aspect of Agumon's personality reflects the Sun's role in providing warmth and life-giving energy.

Conclusion

In "Digital Cosmos: The Astrological Digimon Compendium," Agumon's character serves as a brilliant representation of the Sun's radiant energy and influences. His journey as a Digimon leader, marked by courage, loyalty, strength, and inspiration, mirrors the Sun's role in astrology as a source of vitality, identity, creativity, and leadership. By exploring the parallels between Agumon and the Sun, we gain a deeper appreciation for the ways in which the digital and celestial realms intertwine, enriching our understanding of both Digimon and astrology.

As we continue our exploration of the Digital Cosmos, we will uncover how other Digimon characters embody the qualities of different astrological signs and celestial events, offering new insights into their personalities and adventures. Let Agumon's radiant leadership be our guiding light as we embark on this cosmic journey through the worlds of Digimon and astrology.

Chapter 2: The Moon: Gabumon's Emotional Depth
Characteristics of the Moon in Astrology

The Moon is one of the most significant celestial bodies in astrology, symbolizing our emotions, intuition, and subconscious mind. Unlike the Sun, which represents our external identity and ego, the Moon governs our inner world – our deepest feelings, instincts, and the ways we nurture and seek comfort. It is associated with the water element, which is fluid, reflective, and ever-changing, mirroring the Moon's phases.

Key characteristics of the Moon in astrology include:

- **Emotions and Feelings**: The Moon governs our emotional responses, moods, and how we process feelings.
- **Intuition and Instincts**: It represents our intuitive abilities, gut feelings, and inner guidance.
- **Subconscious Mind**: The Moon is linked to our subconscious thoughts, dreams, and memories.
- **Nurturing and Comfort**: It symbolizes the ways we give and receive care, and how we seek emotional security.
- **Adaptability and Change**: The Moon's phases reflect its dynamic nature, highlighting themes of growth, cycles, and transformation.
- **Connection to the Past**: The Moon often relates to our heritage, family, and ancestral roots.

Gabumon's Role in the Digital World

Gabumon is a beloved Digimon known for his loyalty, sensitivity, and deep emotional bonds with his partner, Matt Ishida. As one of the central characters in the Digimon series, Gabumon plays a crucial role in supporting and guiding Matt through their adventures in the Digital World. Gabumon is characterized by his wolf-like appearance and the fur pelt he wears, which symbolizes his protective and nurturing nature.

Key aspects of Gabumon's role in the Digital World include:

- **Loyalty and Devotion**: Gabumon is fiercely loyal to Matt, providing steadfast support and companionship.
- **Emotional Depth**: He is deeply empathetic and attuned to the emotions of those around him, often acting as a comforting presence.
- **Transformation and Growth**: Gabumon's ability to Digivolve into stronger forms like Garurumon, WereGarurumon, and MetalGarurumon reflects his adaptability and inner strength.
- **Guidance and Intuition**: He often relies on his instincts to navigate challenges, offering intuitive insights to his team.
- **Protectiveness**: Gabumon's protective instincts extend not only to Matt but also to the other DigiDestined and their Digimon partners.

How Gabumon Reflects the Moon's Emotional and Intuitive Qualities

Gabumon's character and actions throughout the Digimon series exemplify the Moon's emotional and intuitive qualities. His journey and interactions provide a rich tapestry that mirrors the lunar themes of nurturing, emotional depth, and intuitive guidance.

1. **Emotions and Feelings**: Gabumon is highly attuned to his own emotions and those of his friends, particularly Matt. He provides emotional support during times of distress, offering a listening ear and comforting presence. Gabumon's sensitivity to emotional undercurrents allows him to connect deeply with others, embodying the Moon's role in governing our feelings and moods.

2. **Intuition and Instincts**: Gabumon often relies on his instincts to guide him and his friends through the Digital World. His intuitive nature helps him sense danger and opportunities, much like the Moon's influence on our gut feelings and inner guidance.

Gabumon's ability to trust his instincts and act on them is a testament to his lunar qualities.

3. **Subconscious Mind**: The Moon's connection to the subconscious mind is reflected in Gabumon's reflective and contemplative nature. He often ponders over past experiences and dreams, drawing insights from them to better understand his journey and his bond with Matt. This introspective quality highlights the Moon's influence on our inner thoughts and memories.

4. **Nurturing and Comfort**: Gabumon's nurturing nature is evident in his interactions with Matt and the other DigiDestined. He provides emotional support, reassurance, and comfort, embodying the Moon's role as a symbol of care and protection. Gabumon's protective instincts ensure that his friends feel safe and loved, reinforcing the lunar theme of seeking and providing emotional security.

5. **Adaptability and Change**: Gabumon's ability to Digivolve into various forms – from Garurumon to MetalGarurumon – mirrors the Moon's dynamic and ever-changing nature. Each evolution represents a new phase of growth and transformation, reflecting the lunar cycle's influence on adaptation and renewal. Gabumon's transformations highlight his resilience and capacity to adapt to new challenges.

6. **Connection to the Past**: Gabumon's connection to his past and heritage is symbolized by the fur pelt he wears. This pelt, which he treasures, serves as a reminder of his roots and the journey he has undertaken. Gabumon's respect for his past and his ability to draw strength from it align with the Moon's role in connecting us to our family and ancestral lineage.

Conclusion

In "Digital Cosmos: The Astrological Digimon Compendium," Gabumon serves as a powerful representation of the Moon's emotional and intuitive qualities. His character, marked by loyalty, sensitivity, and a deep sense of nurturing, mirrors the Moon's influence on our inner world and emotional landscape. Through Gabumon's journey, we gain a deeper appreciation for the ways in which the digital and celestial realms intertwine, offering new insights into the rich tapestry of both Digimon and astrology.

As we continue to explore the Digital Cosmos, we will uncover how other Digimon characters embody the traits and energies of different astrological signs and celestial events. Let Gabumon's emotional depth and intuitive guidance lead us through this cosmic journey, revealing the profound connections between the worlds of Digimon and astrology.

Chapter 3: Mercury: Tentomon's Analytical Mind
Characteristics of Mercury in Astrology

Mercury, named after the Roman messenger god, is the planet of communication, intellect, and reason. It governs our ability to think critically, process information, and convey ideas effectively. In astrology, Mercury influences how we express ourselves, our learning styles, and our capacity for analytical thinking. It rules over the zodiac signs Gemini and Virgo, reflecting dual aspects of communication and meticulous analysis.

Key characteristics of Mercury in astrology include:

- **Communication and Expression**: Mercury governs verbal and written communication, making it easier for us to articulate thoughts and ideas.
- **Intellect and Reasoning**: It influences our intellectual pursuits, logical thinking, and analytical abilities.
- **Adaptability and Versatility**: Mercury's influence promotes adaptability and quick thinking, allowing us to navigate changing circumstances with ease.
- **Curiosity and Learning**: It fuels our curiosity, driving us to seek knowledge and understand the world around us.
- **Trade and Travel**: Mercury is associated with commerce and travel, reflecting the movement and exchange of ideas and goods.
- **Detail Orientation**: Particularly in Virgo, Mercury encourages attention to detail and precision in analysis.

Tentomon's Intelligence and Communication Skills

Tentomon, the insectoid Digimon, is renowned for his intelligence, analytical mind, and excellent communication skills. As the partner Digimon of Izzy Izumi, the group's tech-savvy strategist, Tentomon plays a pivotal role in solving complex problems and deciphering digital anomalies. His inquisitive nature and quick wit make him an invaluable asset to the DigiDestined team.

Key attributes of Tentomon's intelligence and communication skills include:

- **Analytical Thinking**: Tentomon excels at analyzing situations, breaking down problems, and formulating logical solutions.
- **Curiosity and Knowledge**: He has an insatiable curiosity about the Digital World and constantly seeks to expand his knowledge.
- **Technological Proficiency**: Tentomon's proficiency with technology complements Izzy's skills, enabling them to tackle digital challenges effectively.
- **Effective Communication**: He communicates clearly and efficiently, ensuring that his insights and observations are understood by his teammates.
- **Adaptability**: Tentomon quickly adapts to new situations and environments, demonstrating flexibility and resourcefulness.

How Tentomon Represents Mercury's Influence on Intellect and Communication

Tentomon's character and actions throughout the Digimon series vividly illustrate Mercury's influence on intellect and communication. His analytical mind and adeptness at conveying complex ideas make him a perfect embodiment of Mercury's qualities.

1. **Communication and Expression**: Tentomon's ability to articulate his thoughts clearly and concisely reflects Mercury's influence on communication. He often acts as a mediator, explaining intricate digital phenomena to his teammates in an understandable manner. Whether deciphering codes or conveying strategic plans, Tentomon ensures that information flows smoothly within the group.

2. **Intellect and Reasoning**: Tentomon's intellectual prowess is evident in his problem-solving abilities. He approaches challenges with a logical and analytical mindset, much like Mercury's influence on our reasoning capabilities. Tentomon's keen intellect allows him to understand complex digital systems and devise effective solutions, demonstrating Mercury's role in sharpening our mental faculties.

3. **Adaptability and Versatility**: Mercury's adaptability is mirrored in Tentomon's capacity to adjust to various situations. Whether facing new digital threats or exploring unknown territories, Tentomon quickly adapts his strategies to meet the demands of the moment. His versatility is a testament to Mercury's influence on our ability to navigate changing circumstances with ease.

4. **Curiosity and Learning**: Tentomon's insatiable curiosity drives him to constantly seek new knowledge and understand the intricacies of the Digital World. This mirrors Mercury's role in fueling our desire to learn and explore. Tentomon's quest for knowledge often leads to critical discoveries that aid the DigiDestined in their mission, highlighting Mercury's influence on our intellectual growth.

5. **Trade and Travel**: Although not directly related to commerce, Tentomon's role in facilitating the exchange of information and ideas within the group reflects Mercury's association with trade and travel. His ability to gather and disseminate knowledge quickly ensures that the DigiDestined are always well-informed and prepared for their journey.

6. **Detail Orientation**: Tentomon's meticulous attention to detail, particularly when analyzing digital data or solving puzzles, embodies Mercury's influence in Virgo. His precision and thoroughness ensure that no critical information is overlooked, making him a reliable and dependable ally in the Digital World.

Conclusion

In "Digital Cosmos: The Astrological Digimon Compendium," Tentomon serves as a brilliant representation of Mercury's intellectual and communicative qualities. His character, marked by analytical thinking, curiosity, and effective communication, mirrors Mercury's influence on our mental and verbal faculties. Through Tentomon's journey, we gain a deeper appreciation for the ways in which the digital and celestial realms intertwine, enriching our understanding of both Digimon and astrology.

As we continue to explore the Digital Cosmos, we will uncover how other Digimon characters embody the traits and energies of different astrological signs and celestial events. Let Tentomon's analytical mind and communicative prowess guide us through this cosmic journey, revealing the profound connections between the worlds of Digimon and astrology.

Chapter 4: Venus: Biyomon's Harmonious Spirit
Characteristics of Venus in Astrology

Venus, named after the Roman goddess of love and beauty, is the planet of affection, harmony, and aesthetics. It governs our relationships, values, and the ways we experience pleasure and beauty in the world. In astrology, Venus influences how we connect with others, express love, and seek balance and harmony in our lives. It rules over the zodiac signs Taurus and Libra, emphasizing themes of stability, sensuality, social grace, and justice.

Key characteristics of Venus in astrology include:

- **Love and Relationships**: Venus governs romantic and platonic relationships, highlighting our need for connection and affection.
- **Harmony and Balance**: It emphasizes the importance of harmony, balance, and fairness in all areas of life.
- **Beauty and Aesthetics**: Venus is associated with our appreciation of beauty, art, and the finer things in life.
- **Pleasure and Sensuality**: It represents our capacity to experience pleasure, joy, and sensual delights.
- **Values and Desires**: Venus influences our personal values, what we hold dear, and what we desire in life.
- **Social Grace and Diplomacy**: It encourages social harmony, grace, and the ability to navigate relationships with tact and diplomacy.

Biyomon's Loving and Peaceful Nature

Biyomon, the bird-like Digimon, is known for her loving, peaceful, and nurturing nature. As the partner Digimon of Sora Takenouchi, Biyomon plays a vital role in providing emotional support and fostering harmony within the DigiDestined team. Her gentle and compassionate demeanor, coupled with her strong sense of loyalty, makes her a perfect embodiment of Venusian energy.

Key attributes of Biyomon's loving and peaceful nature include:

- **Compassion and Care**: Biyomon is deeply caring and always looks out for her friends, offering comfort and support in times of need.
- **Harmony and Peace**: She strives to maintain peace and harmony within the group, often acting as a mediator in conflicts.
- **Loyalty and Devotion**: Biyomon is fiercely loyal to Sora and the other DigiDestined, demonstrating unwavering dedication and support.
- **Sensitivity and Empathy**: She is highly sensitive to the emotions of those around her and responds with empathy and understanding.
- **Gentleness and Nurturing**: Biyomon's nurturing nature makes her a source of comfort and reassurance, providing a sense of safety and security.

How Biyomon Channels Venus's Energy of Love and Harmony

Biyomon's character and actions throughout the Digimon series vividly illustrate Venus's influence on love, harmony, and beauty. Her gentle nature and commitment to fostering peaceful relationships make her a perfect embodiment of Venus's qualities.

1. **Love and Relationships**: Biyomon's deep bond with Sora exemplifies Venus's influence on love and relationships. Their partnership is characterized by mutual care, respect, and unwavering support. Biyomon's affectionate nature and ability to form strong emotional connections with her friends reflect Venus's role in nurturing love and fostering meaningful relationships.

2. **Harmony and Balance**: Biyomon's efforts to maintain harmony within the DigiDestined team mirror Venus's emphasis on balance and fairness. She often acts as a calming presence during conflicts, helping to resolve disputes and restore peace. Biyomon's dedication to creating a harmonious environment highlights Venus's influence on promoting balance in our interactions.

3. **Beauty and Aesthetics**: While Biyomon's primary focus is on emotional support and harmony, her appreciation for the beauty of the Digital World and its inhabitants reflects Venus's association with aesthetics. Her graceful movements and vibrant appearance embody the beauty and elegance that Venus encourages us to appreciate in life.

4. **Pleasure and Sensuality**: Biyomon's joyful and playful nature aligns with Venus's influence on pleasure and sensuality. She finds delight in simple pleasures and often encourages her friends to enjoy the moment, fostering a sense of joy and contentment. Biyomon's ability to bring happiness and positivity to her surroundings is a testament to Venus's role in enhancing our capacity for pleasure.

5. **Values and Desires**: Biyomon's strong sense of loyalty and dedication to her friends reflects Venus's influence on our values and desires. She prioritizes the well-being of her loved ones and consistently acts in alignment with her core values of love, compassion, and harmony. Biyomon's actions demonstrate how Venus guides us to cherish and uphold what we hold dear.

6. **Social Grace and Diplomacy**: Biyomon's ability to navigate social interactions with grace and diplomacy mirrors Venus's influence on social harmony. She communicates with tact and empathy, ensuring that her words and actions contribute to a peaceful and supportive environment. Biyomon's diplomatic nature helps to strengthen the bonds within the DigiDestined team, fostering unity and cooperation.

Conclusion

In "Digital Cosmos: The Astrological Digimon Compendium," Biyomon serves as a beautiful representation of Venus's qualities of love, harmony, and beauty. Her character, marked by compassion, loyalty, and a nurturing spirit, mirrors Venus's influence on our relationships, values, and capacity for joy. Through Biyomon's journey, we gain a deeper appreciation for the ways in which the digital and celestial realms intertwine, enriching our understanding of both Digimon and astrology.

As we continue to explore the Digital Cosmos, we will uncover how other Digimon characters embody the traits and energies of different astrological signs and celestial events. Let Biyomon's harmonious spirit and loving nature guide us through this cosmic journey, revealing the profound connections between the worlds of Digimon and astrology.

Chapter 5: Mars: Greymon's Warrior Essence
Characteristics of Mars in Astrology

Mars, named after the Roman god of war, is the planet of action, energy, and desire. It governs our drive, determination, and ability to assert ourselves. In astrology, Mars influences how we express our aggression, pursue our goals, and handle challenges. It rules over the zodiac signs Aries and, traditionally, Scorpio, highlighting themes of courage, passion, and transformation.

Key characteristics of Mars in astrology include:

- **Action and Energy**: Mars represents our physical energy and drive to take action.
- **Courage and Determination**: It influences our bravery and tenacity in facing challenges.
- **Aggression and Assertiveness**: Mars governs how we assert ourselves and express our anger.
- **Passion and Desire**: It is associated with our desires, passions, and what motivates us.
- **Competition and Conflict**: Mars is linked to our competitive nature and how we handle conflicts.
- **Initiative and Leadership**: It encourages us to take the lead and initiate actions.

Greymon's Strength and Fighting Spirit

Greymon, the powerful dinosaur Digimon, is renowned for his immense strength, fighting spirit, and unwavering determination. As the Digivolved form of Agumon, Greymon embodies the essence of a warrior, ready to face any challenge head-on. His partnership with Tai Kamiya, the leader of the DigiDestined, further highlights his role as a protector and formidable combatant.

Key attributes of Greymon's strength and fighting spirit include:

- **Physical Power**: Greymon possesses incredible physical strength and combat abilities.
- **Bravery and Valor**: He is courageous and unafraid to confront powerful adversaries.
- **Protectiveness**: Greymon is fiercely protective of his friends and allies, often putting himself in harm's way to ensure their safety.
- **Determination and Tenacity**: He demonstrates relentless determination and perseverance, never giving up in the face of adversity.
- **Aggressiveness in Battle**: Greymon's fighting style is aggressive and forceful, embodying the raw energy of Mars.
- **Leadership in Combat**: As a warrior, Greymon often takes the lead in battles, strategizing and executing powerful attacks.

How Greymon Embodies Mars's Drive and Aggression

Greymon's character and actions throughout the Digimon series vividly illustrate Mars's influence on drive, aggression, and the warrior spirit. His formidable presence and relentless pursuit of victory make him a perfect embodiment of Mars's qualities.

1. **Action and Energy**: Greymon's constant readiness for battle and his ability to take swift, decisive action reflect Mars's influence on our physical energy and drive. Whether charging into combat or launching powerful attacks, Greymon's actions are fueled by a boundless reservoir of energy, mirroring Mars's dynamic and forceful nature.

2. **Courage and Determination**: Greymon's bravery in the face of danger exemplifies Mars's role in fostering courage and determination. He consistently stands up to formidable foes, displaying an unyielding spirit and the willingness to fight for what he be-

lieves in. Greymon's tenacity in overcoming obstacles embodies the Mars-driven determination to achieve victory against all odds.

3. **Aggression and Assertiveness**: Greymon's aggressive combat style and assertive presence are clear manifestations of Mars's influence on aggression and assertiveness. In battle, he unleashes his power with fierce intensity, asserting his dominance and overwhelming his opponents. Greymon's aggressive nature highlights Mars's role in channeling our inner warrior and asserting our will.

4. **Passion and Desire**: Greymon's passion for protecting his friends and his desire to defeat evil resonate with Mars's influence on our deepest desires and motivations. His fierce loyalty and commitment to his allies drive him to push his limits and fight with unwavering fervor. Greymon's passionate spirit mirrors Mars's ability to ignite our inner fire and propel us towards our goals.

5. **Competition and Conflict**: Greymon thrives in competitive and conflict-ridden environments, embodying Mars's association with competition and conflict. His willingness to engage in fierce battles and his drive to emerge victorious underscore Mars's influence on our competitive nature. Greymon's prowess in combat reflects the Mars-driven instinct to confront challenges head-on and dominate adversaries.

6. **Initiative and Leadership**: Greymon's role as a combat leader highlights Mars's encouragement of initiative and leadership. In battles, he often takes the lead, formulating strategies and guiding his teammates to victory. Greymon's leadership in combat situations embodies Mars's influence on our ability to take charge and inspire others through our actions.

Conclusion

In "Digital Cosmos: The Astrological Digimon Compendium," Greymon serves as a powerful representation of Mars's qualities of drive, aggression, and the warrior spirit. His character, marked by physical strength, bravery, and an unyielding determination, mirrors Mars's influence on our actions, desires, and ability to confront challenges. Through Greymon's journey, we gain a deeper appreciation for the ways in which the digital and celestial realms intertwine, enriching our understanding of both Digimon and astrology.

As we continue to explore the Digital Cosmos, we will uncover how other Digimon characters embody the traits and energies of different astrological signs and celestial events. Let Greymon's warrior essence and relentless drive guide us through this cosmic journey, revealing the profound connections between the worlds of Digimon and astrology.

Chapter 6: Jupiter: Leomon's Wise Guidance
Characteristics of Jupiter in Astrology

Jupiter, named after the Roman king of the gods, is the planet of expansion, growth, and wisdom. It represents our higher mind, philosophical thinking, and the pursuit of knowledge. In astrology, Jupiter influences our sense of purpose, optimism, and the desire to explore and understand the world. It governs the zodiac sign Sagittarius and traditionally Pisces, reflecting themes of exploration, spiritual growth, and benevolence.

Key characteristics of Jupiter in astrology include:

- **Expansion and Growth**: Jupiter is associated with growth, abundance, and the desire to expand one's horizons.
- **Wisdom and Knowledge**: It governs higher learning, wisdom, and the quest for understanding and truth.
- **Optimism and Benevolence**: Jupiter embodies optimism, generosity, and a benevolent outlook on life.
- **Philosophical Thinking**: It influences our philosophical and spiritual beliefs, encouraging us to seek deeper meaning.
- **Justice and Morality**: Jupiter is linked to justice, morality, and the pursuit of fairness and ethical principles.
- **Exploration and Adventure**: It encourages exploration, adventure, and the willingness to take risks for the sake of growth.

Leomon's Wisdom and Leadership

Leomon, the lion-like Digimon, is revered for his wisdom, strength, and noble leadership. As a seasoned warrior and mentor, Leomon embodies the essence of a wise guide, offering counsel and support to the

DigiDestined and their partners. His strong sense of justice and unwavering moral compass make him an exemplary figure of Jupiter's expansive and philosophical traits.

Key attributes of Leomon's wisdom and leadership include:

- **Moral Integrity**: Leomon is guided by a strong sense of justice and ethical principles.
- **Mentorship and Guidance**: He provides wisdom and guidance to those in need, often acting as a mentor.
- **Strength and Courage**: Leomon's physical strength is matched by his inner courage and resolve.
- **Sacrifice and Protection**: He is willing to make personal sacrifices to protect others and uphold what is right.
- **Philosophical Insight**: Leomon's understanding of the world is deep and philosophical, reflecting his quest for truth and wisdom.
- **Optimism and Hope**: He maintains a hopeful outlook, inspiring others to stay optimistic even in difficult times.

How Leomon Encapsulates Jupiter's Expansive and Philosophical Traits

Leomon's character and actions throughout the Digimon series vividly illustrate Jupiter's influence on wisdom, expansion, and philosophical thinking. His role as a mentor and protector embodies the benevolent and expansive qualities of Jupiter.

1. **Expansion and Growth**: Leomon's journey and development reflect Jupiter's influence on expansion and growth. He continuously strives to improve himself and expand his understanding of the world. Leomon's ability to grow from his experiences and share that growth with others mirrors Jupiter's role in fostering personal and collective development.

2. **Wisdom and Knowledge**: Leomon's profound wisdom and vast knowledge are clear manifestations of Jupiter's influence. He often imparts valuable lessons and insights to the DigiDestined, guiding them through their challenges with thoughtful advice. Leomon's quest for understanding and his ability to see the bigger picture align with Jupiter's role in governing higher learning and wisdom.

3. **Optimism and Benevolence**: Leomon's optimistic and benevolent nature reflects Jupiter's influence on our outlook on life. Despite the dangers and adversities he faces, Leomon remains hopeful and generous, always ready to help others. His benevolence and positive attitude inspire those around him to maintain hope and strive for a better future.

4. **Philosophical Thinking**: Leomon's deep philosophical insights and reflective nature embody Jupiter's influence on our spiritual and philosophical beliefs. He often contemplates the nature of good and evil, the meaning of courage, and the importance of justice. Leomon's philosophical approach to life encourages the DigiDestined to think deeply about their actions and their impact on the world.

5. **Justice and Morality**: Leomon's unwavering commitment to justice and morality is a testament to Jupiter's influence. He upholds ethical principles and fights for what is right, regardless of the personal cost. Leomon's sense of justice drives him to protect the innocent and confront evil, embodying Jupiter's role in promoting fairness and ethical conduct.

6. **Exploration and Adventure**: Leomon's willingness to embark on adventures and explore new territories reflects Jupiter's association with exploration and risk-taking. He understands that growth and wisdom often come from venturing into the unknown and facing new challenges. Leomon's adventurous spirit encourages others to step out of their comfort zones and embrace the journey of discovery.

Conclusion

In "Digital Cosmos: The Astrological Digimon Compendium," Leomon serves as a powerful representation of Jupiter's qualities of wisdom, expansion, and philosophical thinking. His character, marked by moral integrity, mentorship, and a quest for knowledge, mirrors Jupiter's influence on our growth, optimism, and pursuit of deeper understanding. Through Leomon's journey, we gain a deeper appreciation for the ways in which the digital and celestial realms intertwine, enriching our understanding of both Digimon and astrology.

As we continue to explore the Digital Cosmos, we will uncover how other Digimon characters embody the traits and energies of different astrological signs and celestial events. Let Leomon's wise guidance and expansive spirit lead us through this cosmic journey, revealing the profound connections between the worlds of Digimon and astrology.

Chapter 7: Saturn: Angewomon's Discipline and Structure
Characteristics of Saturn in Astrology

Saturn, named after the Roman god of time and agriculture, is the planet of discipline, responsibility, and structure. It represents the principles of limitation, order, and the need for hard work and perseverance. In astrology, Saturn influences our sense of duty, the challenges we face, and the ways we develop maturity and wisdom through life's trials. It governs the zodiac signs Capricorn and, traditionally, Aquarius, reflecting themes of ambition, practicality, and the pursuit of long-term goals.

Key characteristics of Saturn in astrology include:

- **Discipline and Structure**: Saturn emphasizes the importance of discipline, order, and a structured approach to life.
- **Responsibility and Duty**: It governs our sense of responsibility and our duties towards others and ourselves.
- **Challenges and Hard Work**: Saturn presents challenges and obstacles that require perseverance and hard work to overcome.
- **Maturity and Wisdom**: Through facing difficulties, Saturn helps us develop maturity, wisdom, and a realistic outlook on life.
- **Authority and Boundaries**: Saturn is associated with authority figures, boundaries, and the establishment of rules and regulations.
- **Patience and Long-Term Goals**: It encourages patience, persistence, and the pursuit of long-term achievements.

Angewomon's Role as a Guardian and Enforcer of Justice

Angewomon, the angelic Digimon, is known for her role as a guardian and enforcer of justice. As the Digivolved form of Gatomon, Angewomon embodies purity, righteousness, and unwavering commitment to protecting the innocent and upholding justice. Her presence is both awe-inspiring and reassuring, symbolizing hope and the triumph of good over evil.

Key attributes of Angewomon's role as a guardian and enforcer of justice include:

- **Righteousness and Purity**: Angewomon embodies purity and righteousness, standing as a beacon of hope and virtue.
- **Protectiveness**: She is fiercely protective of her friends and the Digital World, often putting herself at risk to safeguard others.
- **Justice and Fairness**: Angewomon is committed to upholding justice and fairness, ensuring that wrongs are righted and evildoers are held accountable.
- **Wisdom and Guidance**: She provides wisdom and guidance, helping others navigate moral dilemmas and make just decisions.
- **Strength and Resolve**: Angewomon possesses great strength and resolve, demonstrating unwavering determination in the face of adversity.
- **Sacrifice**: She is willing to make personal sacrifices for the greater good, embodying selflessness and duty.

How Angewomon Personifies Saturn's Discipline and Responsibility

Angewomon's character and actions throughout the Digimon series vividly illustrate Saturn's influence on discipline, responsibility, and structure. Her unwavering commitment to justice and her role as a guardian make her a perfect embodiment of Saturn's qualities.

1. **Discipline and Structure**: Angewomon's disciplined approach to her duties and her adherence to a structured moral code reflect Saturn's influence on discipline and order. She operates with a clear sense of purpose and follows a strict code of ethics, ensuring that her actions are always aligned with her principles of justice and righteousness. Angewomon's structured approach to her role as a guardian embodies Saturn's emphasis on order and discipline.

2. **Responsibility and Duty**: Angewomon's strong sense of responsibility and duty is a testament to Saturn's influence. She takes her role as a protector and enforcer of justice very seriously, understanding the weight of her responsibilities. Angewomon's commitment to her duties and her willingness to shoulder burdens for the sake of others highlight Saturn's role in fostering a sense of duty and responsibility.

3. **Challenges and Hard Work**: Throughout her journey, Angewomon faces numerous challenges and adversities. Her ability to overcome these obstacles through perseverance and hard work reflects Saturn's influence on our ability to handle difficulties. Angewomon's resilience and determination in the face of challenges embody Saturn's teachings on the importance of perseverance and effort.

4. **Maturity and Wisdom**: Angewomon's wisdom and maturity are clear manifestations of Saturn's influence. She provides guidance and insight to her friends, helping them navigate complex moral issues and make just decisions. Angewomon's mature outlook and her ability to impart wisdom reflect Saturn's role in fostering growth through experience and challenges.

5. **Authority and Boundaries**: Angewomon's authoritative presence and her ability to establish and enforce boundaries align with Saturn's influence on authority and regulation. She commands respect and ensures that rules and boundaries are upheld, maintaining order and justice within the Digital World. Ange-

woman's role as an enforcer of justice highlights Saturn's association with authority and the establishment of rules.

6. **Patience and Long-Term Goals**: Angewomon's patience and her focus on long-term goals reflect Saturn's influence on persistence and the pursuit of lasting achievements. She understands that true justice and protection require ongoing effort and dedication. Angewomon's commitment to her long-term mission of safeguarding the Digital World embodies Saturn's teachings on patience and perseverance.

Conclusion

In "Digital Cosmos: The Astrological Digimon Compendium," Angewomon serves as a powerful representation of Saturn's qualities of discipline, responsibility, and structure. Her character, marked by righteousness, wisdom, and an unwavering commitment to justice, mirrors Saturn's influence on our sense of duty, perseverance, and the development of maturity through life's challenges. Through Angewomon's journey, we gain a deeper appreciation for the ways in which the digital and celestial realms intertwine, enriching our understanding of both Digimon and astrology.

As we continue to explore the Digital Cosmos, we will uncover how other Digimon characters embody the traits and energies of different astrological signs and celestial events. Let Angewomon's disciplined spirit and responsible nature guide us through this cosmic journey, revealing the profound connections between the worlds of Digimon and astrology.

Chapter 8: Uranus: Patamon's Revolutionary Spirit

Characteristics of Uranus in Astrology

Uranus, named after the Greek god of the sky, is the planet of innovation, rebellion, and sudden changes. It represents the drive for freedom, individuality, and breaking away from the status quo. In astrology, Uranus influences our desire for progress, our ability to think outside the box, and our willingness to embrace the unconventional. It governs the zodiac sign Aquarius, highlighting themes of originality, humanitarianism, and visionary thinking.

Key characteristics of Uranus in astrology include:

- **Innovation and Progress**: Uranus encourages forward-thinking, innovation, and the pursuit of progress and new ideas.
- **Rebellion and Independence**: It governs our rebellious spirit, desire for freedom, and resistance to conformity.
- **Sudden Changes and Surprises**: Uranus is associated with unexpected events, sudden shifts, and breakthroughs.
- **Individuality and Uniqueness**: It emphasizes the importance of individuality, uniqueness, and authenticity.
- **Humanitarianism and Social Reform**: Uranus influences our concern for social issues, humanitarian causes, and the desire to improve society.
- **Visionary Thinking**: It fosters visionary and future-oriented thinking, encouraging us to look beyond the present and imagine new possibilities.

Patamon's Unique Abilities and Unconventional Nature

Patamon, the small, winged Digimon, is known for his unique abilities, unconventional nature, and surprising power. As the partner Digimon of T.K. Takaishi, Patamon plays a crucial role in the adventures of the DigiDestined, often surprising friends and foes alike with his unexpected transformations and abilities. Despite his small size and seemingly gentle demeanor, Patamon possesses a revolutionary spirit that aligns perfectly with Uranus's innovative and rebellious energy.

Key attributes of Patamon's unique abilities and unconventional nature include:

- **Transformation and Evolution**: Patamon's ability to Digivolve into powerful forms like Angemon and MagnaAngemon reflects his capacity for sudden and profound change.
- **Surprising Strength**: Despite his small and unassuming appearance, Patamon possesses remarkable strength and power.
- **Unconventional Approach**: Patamon often employs unconventional strategies and solutions, thinking outside the box to overcome challenges.
- **Courage and Determination**: He demonstrates a fearless spirit and unwavering determination, willing to stand up against formidable adversaries.
- **Gentle and Kind Nature**: Patamon's gentle and kind demeanor contrasts with his powerful abilities, highlighting his unique and multifaceted personality.
- **Adaptability**: Patamon's ability to adapt to various situations and environments reflects his versatile and resilient nature.

How Patamon Reflects Uranus's Innovative and Rebellious Energy

Patamon's character and actions throughout the Digimon series vividly illustrate Uranus's influence on innovation, rebellion, and visionary thinking. His unique abilities, unconventional approach, and surprising strength make him a perfect embodiment of Uranus's qualities.

1. **Innovation and Progress**: Patamon's ability to transform into powerful forms like Angemon and MagnaAngemon represents Uranus's influence on innovation and progress. These transformations are not only surprising but also signify a leap forward in his abilities and strength. Patamon's evolution highlights Uranus's role in fostering groundbreaking advancements and pushing the boundaries of what is possible.

2. **Rebellion and Independence**: Patamon's rebellious spirit is evident in his willingness to challenge powerful adversaries and break free from limitations. His independent nature and resistance to conformity reflect Uranus's influence on our desire for freedom and individuality. Patamon's actions often defy expectations, embodying Uranus's rebellious energy.

3. **Sudden Changes and Surprises**: Patamon's unexpected transformations and surprising abilities are clear manifestations of Uranus's association with sudden changes and surprises. His ability to Digivolve into Angemon during critical moments often takes both allies and enemies by surprise, demonstrating Uranus's influence on sudden shifts and breakthroughs. Patamon's unpredictability keeps his opponents off balance and showcases the power of unexpected change.

4. **Individuality and Uniqueness**: Patamon's unique abilities and distinct personality highlight Uranus's emphasis on individuality and uniqueness. He stands out among the DigiDestined for his gentle demeanor contrasted with his formidable power. Patamon's authenticity and refusal to conform to expectations embody Uranus's encouragement of individuality and self-expression.

5. **Humanitarianism and Social Reform**: Patamon's commitment to protecting his friends and fighting for justice aligns with Uranus's influence on humanitarianism and social reform. He often acts out of a desire to improve the world around him, showing concern for the well-being of others and striving to create a

better future. Patamon's actions reflect Uranus's drive to address social issues and promote positive change.

6. **Visionary Thinking**: Patamon's ability to envision and execute unconventional strategies demonstrates Uranus's influence on visionary thinking. He often approaches challenges with a forward-thinking mindset, imagining new possibilities and innovative solutions. Patamon's visionary approach helps the DigiDestined navigate complex situations and overcome seemingly insurmountable obstacles.

Conclusion

In "Digital Cosmos: The Astrological Digimon Compendium," Patamon serves as a powerful representation of Uranus's qualities of innovation, rebellion, and visionary thinking. His character, marked by unique abilities, unconventional approaches, and surprising strength, mirrors Uranus's influence on our drive for progress, individuality, and social reform. Through Patamon's journey, we gain a deeper appreciation for the ways in which the digital and celestial realms intertwine, enriching our understanding of both Digimon and astrology.

As we continue to explore the Digital Cosmos, we will uncover how other Digimon characters embody the traits and energies of different astrological signs and celestial events. Let Patamon's revolutionary spirit and innovative energy guide us through this cosmic journey, revealing the profound connections between the worlds of Digimon and astrology.

Chapter 9: Neptune: Gatomon's Mystical Influence
Characteristics of Neptune in Astrology

Neptune, named after the Roman god of the sea, is the planet of dreams, intuition, and spirituality. It represents the realm of the unseen, the subconscious, and the mystical. In astrology, Neptune influences our imagination, compassion, and our connection to the divine and the ethereal. It governs the zodiac sign Pisces, reflecting themes of empathy, creativity, and transcendence.

Key characteristics of Neptune in astrology include:

- **Dreams and Imagination**: Neptune governs our dreams, fantasies, and the creative power of our imagination.
- **Intuition and Psychic Abilities**: It enhances our intuitive and psychic abilities, allowing us to connect with deeper, unseen realms.
- **Spirituality and Mysticism**: Neptune influences our spiritual beliefs and practices, encouraging us to seek a higher connection and understanding.
- **Compassion and Empathy**: It fosters deep compassion, empathy, and a desire to help others.
- **Illusion and Deception**: Neptune can also bring about illusions, deception, and a lack of clarity, blurring the lines between reality and fantasy.
- **Transcendence and Dissolution**: It represents the dissolution of boundaries and the transcendence of the material world.

Gatomon's Mysterious and Spiritual Qualities

Gatomon, the feline Digimon, is known for her mysterious, spiritual, and compassionate nature. As the partner Digimon of Kari Kamiya, Gatomon possesses a deep sense of intuition and a strong connection to the spiritual realm. Her journey from a dark past to becoming a guardian of light highlights her mystical qualities and her capacity for empathy and transformation.

Key attributes of Gatomon's mysterious and spiritual qualities include:

- **Intuitive Insight**: Gatomon has a keen sense of intuition, often sensing danger and understanding situations on a deeper level.
- **Mystical Abilities**: Her powers, particularly when she Digivolves into Angewomon, are imbued with a mystical and divine energy.
- **Empathy and Compassion**: Gatomon shows profound empathy and compassion, especially towards those who are suffering or in need of help.
- **Spiritual Connection**: Her bond with Kari is deeply spiritual, reflecting a higher connection and purpose.
- **Transformation and Redemption**: Gatomon's transformation from a servant of darkness to a warrior of light embodies themes of redemption and spiritual growth.
- **Protectiveness and Healing**: She is protective of her friends and possesses healing abilities that provide comfort and support.

How Gatomon Embodies Neptune's Mystical and Compassionate Essence

Gatomon's character and actions throughout the Digimon series vividly illustrate Neptune's influence on mysticism, compassion, and spirituality. Her intuitive insights, mystical powers, and deep empathy make her a perfect embodiment of Neptune's qualities.

1. **Dreams and Imagination**: Gatomon's journey and transformation reflect Neptune's influence on dreams and imagination. Her past is filled with dark dreams and illusions, but through her bond with Kari and the DigiDestined, she finds a path to light and redemption. Gatomon's ability to envision a better future and transform her reality mirrors Neptune's power to inspire and elevate our dreams.

2. **Intuition and Psychic Abilities**: Gatomon's keen intuition and psychic-like abilities are clear manifestations of Neptune's influence. She often senses danger before it occurs and has a deep understanding of the emotional and spiritual states of those around her. Gatomon's intuitive insights guide her and her friends, embodying Neptune's enhancement of our psychic faculties.

3. **Spirituality and Mysticism**: Gatomon's spiritual nature is most evident when she Digivolves into Angewomon, a form imbued with divine and mystical energy. Her connection to the spiritual realm and her role as a guardian of light reflect Neptune's influence on our spiritual beliefs and practices. Gatomon's journey towards enlightenment and her divine powers symbolize Neptune's role in guiding us towards higher spiritual understanding.

4. **Compassion and Empathy**: Gatomon's deep compassion and empathy align with Neptune's influence on our capacity for kindness and understanding. She often reaches out to those in need, offering comfort and support. Gatomon's empathetic nature and her desire to help others highlight Neptune's role in fostering deep emotional connections and selfless love.

5. **Illusion and Deception**: Gatomon's past under the influence of Myotismon is marked by deception and illusions, reflecting Neptune's potential for blurring reality and fantasy. Her ability to break free from these illusions and find clarity and truth demonstrates Neptune's dual nature – the challenge of overcoming deception to achieve spiritual enlightenment.

6. **Transcendence and Dissolution**: Gatomon's transformation and redemption story embodies Neptune's theme of transcendence and the dissolution of boundaries. Her journey from darkness to light represents the transcendence of past limitations and the dissolution of her former self. Gatomon's ability to overcome her past and embrace a higher purpose highlights Neptune's influence on spiritual growth and transformation.

Conclusion

In "Digital Cosmos: The Astrological Digimon Compendium," Gatomon serves as a profound representation of Neptune's qualities of mysticism, compassion, and spirituality. Her character, marked by intuitive insight, spiritual connection, and deep empathy, mirrors Neptune's influence on our dreams, intuition, and desire for transcendence. Through Gatomon's journey, we gain a deeper appreciation for the ways in which the digital and celestial realms intertwine, enriching our understanding of both Digimon and astrology.

As we continue to explore the Digital Cosmos, we will uncover how other Digimon characters embody the traits and energies of different astrological signs and celestial events. Let Gatomon's mystical influence and compassionate spirit guide us through this cosmic journey, revealing the profound connections between the worlds of Digimon and astrology.

Chapter 10: Pluto: Beelzemon's Transformative Power
Characteristics of Pluto in Astrology

Pluto, named after the Roman god of the underworld, is the planet of transformation, power, and rebirth. It governs the processes of destruction and regeneration, symbolizing profound change and the emergence of new beginnings from the ashes of the old. In astrology, Pluto influences our deepest drives, our capacity for profound transformation, and our relationship with power and control. It rules the zodiac sign Scorpio, emphasizing themes of intensity, secrecy, and the cycle of life, death, and rebirth.

Key characteristics of Pluto in astrology include:

- **Transformation and Rebirth**: Pluto represents the process of profound change and the cycle of death and rebirth.
- **Power and Control**: It governs issues of power, control, and the dynamics of dominance and submission.
- **Depth and Intensity**: Pluto is associated with deep, intense emotions and experiences.
- **Secrets and the Unconscious**: It influences the hidden aspects of our psyche, including our unconscious drives and fears.
- **Regeneration and Healing**: Pluto's transformative power also brings the potential for healing and regeneration.
- **Obsession and Compulsion**: It can manifest as obsessive and compulsive behaviors, highlighting our deepest desires and fears.

Beelzemon's Journey of Transformation and Redemption

Beelzemon, originally known as Impmon, undergoes one of the most profound and compelling journeys of transformation and redemption in the Digimon series. Starting as a mischievous and somewhat malevolent character, Impmon's quest for power leads him down a dark path. However, through a series of intense experiences and realizations, he ultimately seeks redemption and transforms into a powerful but reformed Digimon.

Key aspects of Beelzemon's journey of transformation and redemption include:

- **Desire for Power**: Impmon's initial transformation into Beelzemon is driven by his intense desire for power and recognition.
- **Descent into Darkness**: His quest for power leads him to make dark choices, aligning with the forces of evil and causing harm to others.
- **Realization and Guilt**: Beelzemon eventually realizes the consequences of his actions, experiencing profound guilt and remorse.
- **Quest for Redemption**: Seeking to atone for his past, Beelzemon embarks on a journey of redemption, protecting those he once harmed and fighting for justice.
- **Transformation and Rebirth**: His transformation from Impmon to Beelzemon, and later to Beelzemon Blast Mode, symbolizes his rebirth and the profound change in his character.
- **Power and Responsibility**: Beelzemon learns to wield his immense power responsibly, embodying the potential for regeneration and healing.

How Beelzemon Represents Pluto's Themes of Power, Transformation, and Rebirth

Beelzemon's character arc throughout the Digimon series vividly illustrates Pluto's influence on power, transformation, and rebirth. His journey from a power-hungry Digimon to a redeemed warrior embodies the profound and often painful process of change and regeneration that Pluto governs.

1. **Transformation and Rebirth**: Beelzemon's journey is a quintessential representation of Pluto's theme of transformation and

rebirth. His evolution from Impmon to Beelzemon, and later to Beelzemon Blast Mode, symbolizes the death of his old self and the rebirth of a new, more enlightened being. This transformation is marked by profound inner change and the emergence of new strengths and insights.

2. **Power and Control**: Beelzemon's initial desire for power and his subsequent struggle with its consequences reflect Pluto's influence on power and control. His journey highlights the destructive potential of unchecked power and the importance of learning to control and wield it responsibly. Beelzemon's eventual mastery over his power embodies Pluto's lesson that true strength lies in self-control and the ethical use of power.

3. **Depth and Intensity**: Beelzemon's experiences are marked by intense emotions and deep psychological challenges, mirroring Pluto's association with depth and intensity. His feelings of guilt, remorse, and the drive for redemption are profound and transformative, reflecting the deep emotional currents that Pluto stirs within us.

4. **Secrets and the Unconscious**: Beelzemon's journey delves into the hidden aspects of his psyche, including his fears, desires, and the darker sides of his personality. This exploration of his unconscious drives and the uncovering of his true potential align with Pluto's influence on the secrets and depths of our inner world.

5. **Regeneration and Healing**: Beelzemon's quest for redemption and his eventual transformation into a protector and hero symbolize Pluto's potential for regeneration and healing. Despite the destruction he once caused, Beelzemon is able to heal and regenerate, both within himself and in his relationships with others. His story highlights the possibility of profound healing and the renewal that can arise from facing and overcoming our darkest challenges.

6. **Obsession and Compulsion**: Beelzemon's initial obsession with power and recognition drives much of his early behavior, reflect-

ing Pluto's influence on obsession and compulsion. His journey shows the dangers of allowing these drives to dominate us, but also the potential for transformation when we confront and transcend them.

Conclusion

In "Digital Cosmos: The Astrological Digimon Compendium," Beelzemon serves as a powerful representation of Pluto's qualities of transformation, power, and rebirth. His character, marked by profound change, the struggle for control, and the quest for redemption, mirrors Pluto's influence on our deepest drives and the potential for profound transformation. Through Beelzemon's journey, we gain a deeper appreciation for the ways in which the digital and celestial realms intertwine, enriching our understanding of both Digimon and astrology.

As we continue to explore the Digital Cosmos, we will uncover how other Digimon characters embody the traits and energies of different astrological signs and celestial events. Let Beelzemon's transformative power and journey of redemption guide us through this cosmic journey, revealing the profound connections between the worlds of Digimon and astrology.

Part 2: Zodiac Signs and Their Digital Avatars

Chapter 11: Aries: Veemon's Fiery Determination
Characteristics of Aries in Astrology

Aries, the first sign of the zodiac, is ruled by Mars and symbolizes the dawn of new beginnings. It represents the pioneering spirit, assertiveness, and the drive to initiate and conquer. Aries is associated with the fire element, reflecting its passionate, dynamic, and sometimes impulsive nature. People influenced by Aries are often seen as courageous leaders, ready to face challenges head-on and blaze new trails.

Key characteristics of Aries in astrology include:

- **Assertiveness and Initiative**: Aries is known for its proactive approach, always eager to take the lead and start new projects.
- **Courage and Boldness**: The sign embodies bravery and a fearless attitude, willing to confront obstacles and take risks.
- **Passion and Enthusiasm**: Aries individuals are highly enthusiastic and energetic, infusing their pursuits with a fiery passion.
- **Independence and Self-Reliance**: They value their independence and often prefer to rely on themselves to achieve their goals.
- **Competitiveness and Drive**: Aries is highly competitive, always striving to be the best and achieve victory.
- **Impulsiveness and Quick Action**: Their eagerness can sometimes lead to impulsive decisions, driven by the desire for immediate action.

Veemon's Dynamic and Courageous Nature

Veemon, the dragon-like Digimon, is known for his dynamic, courageous, and determined personality. As the partner Digimon of Davis Motomiya, Veemon embodies the spirit of a true warrior, always ready to face challenges and protect his friends. His evolution into various powerful forms, such as ExVeemon and Imperialdramon, highlights his potential for growth and transformation.

Key attributes of Veemon's dynamic and courageous nature include:

- **Bravery and Fearlessness**: Veemon is always willing to confront danger, no matter how formidable the foe.
- **Energetic and Enthusiastic**: He approaches every situation with boundless energy and enthusiasm.
- **Loyalty and Protectiveness**: Veemon is fiercely loyal to Davis and the other DigiDestined, always putting their safety above his own.
- **Determination and Persistence**: He never gives up, regardless of the challenges he faces, showing an unyielding determination.
- **Combat Skills and Strength**: Veemon possesses impressive combat abilities, making him a formidable opponent in battle.
- **Adaptability and Growth**: His ability to evolve into various powerful forms reflects his potential for growth and adaptation.

How Veemon Channels Aries's Assertive and Pioneering Spirit

Veemon's character and actions throughout the Digimon series vividly illustrate Aries's influence on assertiveness, courage, and pioneering spirit. His dynamic presence and relentless drive make him a perfect embodiment of Aries's qualities.

1. **Assertiveness and Initiative**: Veemon's proactive nature and eagerness to take action reflect Aries's assertiveness and initiative. He often takes the lead in battles, charging forward without hesitation and inspiring his friends to follow suit. Veemon's readiness to initiate action and confront challenges head-on embodies Aries's pioneering spirit.
2. **Courage and Boldness**: Veemon's bravery in the face of danger exemplifies Aries's courage and boldness. He confronts powerful adversaries with fearless determination, demonstrating the fearless attitude that defines Aries. Veemon's willingness to take risks and stand up against overwhelming odds highlights Aries's role as the courageous warrior.

3. **Passion and Enthusiasm**: Veemon's energetic and enthusiastic approach to every situation mirrors Aries's passion and zest for life. His excitement and drive to protect his friends and achieve victory infuse his actions with a fiery intensity. Veemon's enthusiasm inspires those around him, reflecting Aries's ability to ignite passion in others.

4. **Independence and Self-Reliance**: Veemon's independent nature and self-reliance align with Aries's value of independence. While he works well with the DigiDestined team, he also shows a strong sense of personal responsibility and capability. Veemon's confidence in his abilities and his readiness to tackle challenges on his own embody Aries's self-reliant spirit.

5. **Competitiveness and Drive**: Veemon's competitive nature and relentless drive to succeed are clear manifestations of Aries's influence. He constantly pushes himself to improve and evolve, striving to become stronger and more capable. Veemon's determination to be the best and achieve his goals reflects Aries's competitive and ambitious nature.

6. **Impulsiveness and Quick Action**: Veemon's tendency to act quickly and sometimes impulsively demonstrates Aries's impulsive energy. While his quick actions can sometimes lead to hasty decisions, they also enable him to respond rapidly to threats and seize opportunities. Veemon's readiness to act on instinct and his swift response to challenges embody Aries's quick and decisive nature.

Conclusion

In "Digital Cosmos: The Astrological Digimon Compendium," Veemon serves as a powerful representation of Aries's qualities of assertiveness, courage, and pioneering spirit. His character, marked by dynamic energy, fearless determination, and a relentless drive to succeed, mirrors Aries's influence on our actions, desires, and leadership capabilities. Through Veemon's journey, we gain a deeper appreciation for the ways in which the digital and celestial realms intertwine, enriching our understanding of both Digimon and astrology.

As we continue to explore the Digital Cosmos, we will uncover how other Digimon characters embody the traits and energies of different astrological signs and celestial events. Let Veemon's fiery determination and pioneering spirit guide us through this cosmic journey, revealing the profound connections between the worlds of Digimon and astrology.

Chapter 12: Taurus: Palmon's Steady Growth
Characteristics of Taurus in Astrology

Taurus, the second sign of the zodiac, is ruled by Venus and symbolizes stability, persistence, and the pleasures of the material world. Represented by the bull, Taurus is associated with the earth element, reflecting its grounded, reliable, and practical nature. People influenced by Taurus are often seen as patient, nurturing, and deeply connected to the physical world, valuing comfort, beauty, and steady progress.

Key characteristics of Taurus in astrology include:

- **Stability and Reliability**: Taurus is known for its dependable and steadfast nature, providing a sense of security and consistency.
- **Patience and Persistence**: It embodies patience and persistence, steadily working towards goals without rushing.
- **Connection to Nature**: Taurus has a deep appreciation for nature and the natural world, finding joy in the beauty and tranquility of the environment.
- **Nurturing and Sensuality**: It is associated with nurturing qualities and a love for sensory pleasures, including food, art, and physical comfort.
- **Practicality and Groundedness**: Taurus is practical and realistic, focusing on tangible results and concrete achievements.
- **Value of Material Comfort**: It values material comfort and security, seeking to create a stable and comfortable environment.

Palmon's Connection to Nature and Growth

Palmon, the plant-like Digimon, is known for her deep connection to nature, her nurturing personality, and her steady growth. As the partner Digimon of Mimi Tachikawa, Palmon plays a crucial role in the adventures of the DigiDestined, often providing support and healing to her friends. Her evolution into Togemon and later into Lillymon highlights her capacity for growth and transformation, always rooted in her connection to the natural world.

Key attributes of Palmon's connection to nature and growth include:

- **Nurturing and Healing**: Palmon possesses healing abilities and often takes care of her friends, providing comfort and support.
- **Growth and Transformation**: Her ability to evolve into stronger forms like Togemon and Lillymon reflects her steady growth and potential for transformation.
- **Patience and Persistence**: Palmon is patient and persistent, often working diligently to overcome challenges.
- **Grounded and Practical**: She has a practical approach to problems, finding grounded and realistic solutions.
- **Love for Nature**: Palmon's very being is intertwined with nature, embodying its beauty, resilience, and regenerative qualities.
- **Stability and Support**: She provides a stable and reliable presence, offering her steadfast support to the DigiDestined.

How Palmon Embodies Taurus's Stability and Nurturing Qualities

Palmon's character and actions throughout the Digimon series vividly illustrate Taurus's influence on stability, nurturing, and growth. Her deep connection to nature, patient demeanor, and steady development make her a perfect embodiment of Taurus's qualities.

1. **Stability and Reliability**: Palmon's dependable nature and consistent support reflect Taurus's stability and reliability. She is always there for her friends, providing a steady presence and offering her assistance whenever needed. Palmon's unwavering support embodies Taurus's role as a reliable and stable influence.
2. **Patience and Persistence**: Palmon's patient and persistent approach to challenges exemplifies Taurus's patience and determi-

nation. She doesn't rush into situations but carefully and diligently works towards her goals. Palmon's persistence in overcoming obstacles mirrors Taurus's ability to achieve success through steady effort and perseverance.

3. **Connection to Nature**: Palmon's deep connection to nature is a clear manifestation of Taurus's affinity with the natural world. Her plant-like appearance and abilities highlight her bond with the environment, reflecting Taurus's appreciation for the beauty and tranquility of nature. Palmon's connection to the earth and her ability to draw strength from it align with Taurus's grounded nature.

4. **Nurturing and Sensuality**: Palmon's nurturing personality and her role as a healer reflect Taurus's nurturing and sensual qualities. She often provides comfort and care to her friends, helping them recover and find solace. Palmon's love for beauty and her ability to bring a sense of peace and well-being to those around her embody Taurus's nurturing spirit.

5. **Practicality and Groundedness**: Palmon's practical and grounded approach to problems aligns with Taurus's practicality and realism. She finds tangible solutions and focuses on what can be realistically achieved. Palmon's grounded nature ensures that her actions are effective and rooted in reality, reflecting Taurus's pragmatic outlook.

6. **Value of Material Comfort**: While Palmon's primary focus is on her connection to nature, her desire to create a stable and comfortable environment for her friends aligns with Taurus's value of material comfort and security. She strives to ensure that those around her feel safe and cared for, reflecting Taurus's emphasis on creating a nurturing and secure atmosphere.

Conclusion

In "Digital Cosmos: The Astrological Digimon Compendium," Palmon serves as a beautiful representation of Taurus's qualities of stability, nurturing, and steady growth. Her character, marked by a deep connection to nature, patient persistence, and a nurturing spirit, mirrors Taurus's influence on our actions, values, and relationships. Through Palmon's journey, we gain a deeper appreciation for the ways in which the digital and celestial realms intertwine, enriching our understanding of both Digimon and astrology.

As we continue to explore the Digital Cosmos, we will uncover how other Digimon characters embody the traits and energies of different astrological signs and celestial events. Let Palmon's steady growth and nurturing qualities guide us through this cosmic journey, revealing the profound connections between the worlds of Digimon and astrology.

Chapter 13: Gemini: Lopmon's Dual Nature
Characteristics of Gemini in Astrology

Gemini, the third sign of the zodiac, is ruled by Mercury and symbolizes duality, communication, and adaptability. Represented by the twins, Gemini is associated with the air element, reflecting its intellectual, versatile, and sociable nature. People influenced by Gemini are often seen as curious, quick-witted, and able to see multiple perspectives, valuing knowledge, interaction, and mental stimulation.

Key characteristics of Gemini in astrology include:

- **Duality and Versatility**: Gemini is known for its dual nature, capable of adapting to different situations and embodying various roles.
- **Communication and Expression**: It governs communication, making Gemini individuals adept at expressing themselves and connecting with others.
- **Curiosity and Learning**: Gemini has an insatiable curiosity and a love for learning and acquiring new information.
- **Sociability and Interaction**: It values social interactions and thrives in environments where ideas and conversations flow freely.
- **Intellectual and Analytical**: Gemini is intellectually driven, enjoying mental challenges and analytical thinking.
- **Restlessness and Changeability**: Gemini's restless nature makes it prone to seeking change and variety, avoiding routine and monotony.

Lopmon's Adaptability and Duality

Lopmon, the rabbit-like Digimon, is known for her adaptability, dual nature, and gentle demeanor. As the partner Digimon of Suzie Wong in Digimon Tamers, and previously of Willis in Digimon: The Movie, Lopmon showcases a remarkable capacity to switch between contrasting roles and forms, such as her darker counterpart Antylamon and her ultimate form Cherubimon. Her journey highlights her versatility, communicative abilities, and the inherent duality of her character.

Key attributes of Lopmon's adaptability and duality include:

- **Transformation and Dual Forms**: Lopmon's ability to transform into Antylamon and Cherubimon demonstrates her dual nature and adaptability.
- **Gentleness and Strength**: She possesses a gentle and nurturing personality, balanced with the strength and power of her evolved forms.
- **Communication and Connection**: Lopmon communicates effectively with her partners and other Digimon, forming strong emotional bonds.
- **Curiosity and Exploration**: She shows a curious nature, eager to explore and learn from her surroundings.
- **Flexibility and Resourcefulness**: Lopmon adapts to various situations with ease, showcasing resourcefulness and versatility.
- **Balancing Contrasts**: She embodies the balance between light and dark, strength and gentleness, highlighting her dual nature.

How Lopmon Reflects Gemini's Versatility and Communicative Skills

Lopmon's character and actions throughout the Digimon series vividly illustrate Gemini's influence on versatility, communication, and adaptability. Her dual nature, communicative abilities, and intellectual curiosity make her a perfect embodiment of Gemini's qualities.

1. **Duality and Versatility**: Lopmon's dual nature is the essence of Gemini's characteristic duality and versatility. Her ability to transform into Antylamon, a more powerful and darker form, and eventually into Cherubimon, a form of great wisdom and light, highlights her capacity to embody different roles and adapt to changing circumstances. Lopmon's versatility in shifting between these forms mirrors Gemini's ability to navigate various facets of life and personality.

2. **Communication and Expression**: Lopmon's effective communication and strong emotional connections with her partners reflect Gemini's influence on communication and expression. She forms deep bonds with Suzie and Willis, understanding their needs and providing guidance and support. Lopmon's communicative skills and her ability to connect with others embody Gemini's talent for expressing thoughts and feelings clearly and empathetically.

3. **Curiosity and Learning**: Lopmon's curious nature and eagerness to explore new environments and learn from her experiences align with Gemini's love for learning and intellectual stimulation. Her journey is marked by a constant quest for understanding and growth, reflecting Gemini's insatiable curiosity and drive for knowledge. Lopmon's willingness to explore and adapt to new situations embodies Gemini's intellectual curiosity.

4. **Sociability and Interaction**: Lopmon's sociable and interactive nature highlights Gemini's value of social connections and interactions. She thrives in environments where she can engage with others, share ideas, and form meaningful relationships. Lopmon's sociability and her ability to navigate social dynamics effectively reflect Gemini's sociable and communicative spirit.

5. **Intellectual and Analytical**: Lopmon's analytical thinking and problem-solving abilities showcase Gemini's intellectual and analytical traits. She approaches challenges with a keen mind, finding solutions through careful thought and analysis. Lopmon's intel-

lectual capabilities and her strategic approach to overcoming obstacles embody Gemini's analytical prowess.

6. **Restlessness and Changeability**: Lopmon's adaptability and ability to embrace change align with Gemini's restlessness and desire for variety. She is not bound by routine and can quickly adjust to new circumstances, showcasing flexibility and resilience. Lopmon's readiness to adapt and her comfort with change reflect Gemini's dynamic and changeable nature.

Conclusion

In "Digital Cosmos: The Astrological Digimon Compendium," Lopmon serves as a powerful representation of Gemini's qualities of versatility, communication, and duality. Her character, marked by adaptability, intellectual curiosity, and strong communicative skills, mirrors Gemini's influence on our actions, thoughts, and relationships. Through Lopmon's journey, we gain a deeper appreciation for the ways in which the digital and celestial realms intertwine, enriching our understanding of both Digimon and astrology.

As we continue to explore the Digital Cosmos, we will uncover how other Digimon characters embody the traits and energies of different astrological signs and celestial events. Let Lopmon's dual nature and versatile spirit guide us through this cosmic journey, revealing the profound connections between the worlds of Digimon and astrology.

Chapter 14: Cancer: Gomamon's Protective Instincts

Characteristics of Cancer in Astrology

Cancer, the fourth sign of the zodiac, is ruled by the Moon and symbolizes emotions, home, and family. Represented by the crab, Cancer is associated with the water element, reflecting its deep, intuitive, and nurturing nature. People influenced by Cancer are often seen as empathetic, caring, and protective, valuing emotional connections, security, and the well-being of their loved ones.

Key characteristics of Cancer in astrology include:

- **Emotional Sensitivity**: Cancer is deeply in touch with their emotions and those of others, often acting with empathy and compassion.
- **Nurturing and Caring**: It embodies nurturing qualities, always seeking to care for and protect their loved ones.
- **Intuition and Insight**: Cancer has a strong intuitive sense, often understanding situations and people on a deeper level.
- **Protectiveness and Security**: It values security and is fiercely protective of their home and family.
- **Connection to Home and Family**: Cancer places great importance on home and family, finding comfort and strength in these connections.
- **Moody and Changeable**: Influenced by the Moon, Cancer's moods can fluctuate, reflecting the ever-changing nature of their emotions.

Gomamon's Caring and Protective Nature

Gomamon, the aquatic Digimon, is known for his caring, playful, and protective nature. As the partner Digimon of Joe Kido, Gomamon plays a crucial role in supporting and safeguarding his friends. His ability to summon aquatic creatures and his adaptability to different environments highlight his deep connection to water and his nurturing instincts.

Key attributes of Gomamon's caring and protective nature include:

- **Protectiveness**: Gomamon is fiercely protective of Joe and the other DigiDestined, always ready to defend them from danger.
- **Playfulness and Cheerfulness**: Despite his protective instincts, Gomamon maintains a playful and cheerful demeanor, bringing joy to his friends.
- **Empathy and Understanding**: He shows a deep understanding of his friends' emotions, often providing comfort and support.
- **Adaptability**: Gomamon's ability to thrive in various environments, particularly water, reflects his adaptable and resilient nature.
- **Nurturing**: He cares for his friends, ensuring their well-being and offering encouragement during tough times.
- **Resourcefulness**: Gomamon uses his abilities creatively to solve problems and protect his companions.

How Gomamon Channels Cancer's Nurturing and Empathetic Energy

Gomamon's character and actions throughout the Digimon series vividly illustrate Cancer's influence on nurturing, empathy, and protection. His caring demeanor, intuitive understanding, and protective instincts make him a perfect embodiment of Cancer's qualities.

1. **Emotional Sensitivity**: Gomamon's ability to sense and respond to the emotions of his friends reflects Cancer's deep emotional sensitivity. He often provides comfort and reassurance when they are feeling down or anxious. Gomamon's empathetic nature allows him to connect with others on an emotional level, embodying Cancer's compassionate spirit.

2. **Nurturing and Caring**: Gomamon's nurturing personality is a clear manifestation of Cancer's caring qualities. He takes care of his friends, ensuring they are safe and supported. Whether it's offering words of encouragement or physically defending them, Gomamon's actions highlight Cancer's instinct to nurture and protect.

3. **Intuition and Insight**: Gomamon's intuitive understanding of situations and people aligns with Cancer's strong intuitive sense. He often anticipates dangers and understands the underlying emotions of his friends, guiding them with insight and wisdom. Gomamon's ability to navigate complex emotional landscapes reflects Cancer's intuitive and insightful nature.

4. **Protectiveness and Security**: Gomamon's protective instincts are a testament to Cancer's value of security and protection. He is always vigilant, ready to defend his friends from any threat. Gomamon's determination to keep his loved ones safe embodies Cancer's fierce protectiveness and dedication to providing security.

5. **Connection to Home and Family**: Gomamon's bond with Joe and the other DigiDestined mirrors Cancer's deep connection to home and family. He views his friends as his family and is deeply committed to their well-being. Gomamon's loyalty and dedication to his companions highlight Cancer's emphasis on the importance of family and close-knit relationships.

6. **Moody and Changeable**: Gomamon's playful and cheerful demeanor can sometimes shift to a more serious and protective stance, reflecting Cancer's moody and changeable nature. Influenced by the ever-changing Moon, Gomamon's ability to adapt his behavior to suit the needs of the moment showcases Cancer's dynamic emotional landscape.

Conclusion

In "Digital Cosmos: The Astrological Digimon Compendium," Gomamon serves as a powerful representation of Cancer's qualities of nurturing, empathy, and protection. His character, marked by emotional sensitivity, caring instincts, and a deep connection to his friends, mirrors Cancer's influence on our actions, values, and relationships. Through Gomamon's journey, we gain a deeper appreciation for the ways in which the digital and celestial realms intertwine, enriching our understanding of both Digimon and astrology.

As we continue to explore the Digital Cosmos, we will uncover how other Digimon characters embody the traits and energies of different astrological signs and celestial events. Let Gomamon's protective instincts and nurturing energy guide us through this cosmic journey, revealing the profound connections between the worlds of Digimon and astrology.

Chapter 15: Leo: Coronamon's Regal Presence
Characteristics of Leo in Astrology

Leo, the fifth sign of the zodiac, is ruled by the Sun and symbolizes leadership, creativity, and self-expression. Represented by the lion, Leo is associated with the fire element, reflecting its passionate, dynamic, and charismatic nature. People influenced by Leo are often seen as confident, generous, and natural-born leaders, valuing recognition, loyalty, and the pursuit of their creative passions.

Key characteristics of Leo in astrology include:

- **Charisma and Confidence**: Leo is known for its magnetic personality, exuding confidence and charm.
- **Leadership and Authority**: It embodies natural leadership qualities, often taking charge and inspiring others.
- **Creativity and Self-Expression**: Leo is highly creative, seeking to express themselves through various forms of art and performance.
- **Generosity and Warmth**: It is generous and warm-hearted, always willing to share and support others.
- **Pride and Honor**: Leo values pride and honor, striving to maintain their dignity and reputation.
- **Loyalty and Protection**: It is fiercely loyal and protective of their loved ones, ensuring their safety and well-being.

Coronamon's Pride and Leadership

Coronamon, the lion-like Digimon, is known for his pride, leadership, and dynamic presence. As the partner Digimon of Marcus Damon in Digimon Data Squad, Coronamon exhibits traits that align closely with the characteristics of Leo. His ability to evolve into Firamon and ultimately Apollomon highlights his regal and powerful nature, making him a natural leader and protector.

Key attributes of Coronamon's pride and leadership include:

- **Pride and Self-Respect**: Coronamon holds himself with great pride, maintaining a sense of dignity and self-respect.
- **Leadership**: He naturally takes on leadership roles, guiding and inspiring his allies in battles and missions.
- **Courage and Bravery**: Coronamon is fearless in the face of danger, always ready to confront threats head-on.
- **Generosity and Support**: He is generous with his strength and support, always willing to lend a hand to his friends.
- **Creativity and Passion**: Coronamon exhibits a passionate approach to his missions, often finding creative ways to overcome challenges.
- **Loyalty and Protection**: He is fiercely loyal to Marcus and his companions, protecting them with unwavering dedication.

How Coronamon Embodies Leo's Charismatic and Confident Traits

Coronamon's character and actions throughout the Digimon series vividly illustrate Leo's influence on charisma, confidence, and leadership. His dynamic presence, courageous spirit, and generous nature make him a perfect embodiment of Leo's qualities.

1. **Charisma and Confidence**: Coronamon's magnetic personality and confident demeanor reflect Leo's charismatic and confident traits. He exudes a natural charm that draws others to him, inspiring trust and admiration. Coronamon's self-assured nature allows him to tackle challenges with poise, embodying Leo's confident spirit.

2. **Leadership and Authority**: Coronamon's ability to take charge and lead his allies in battle showcases Leo's natural leadership qualities. He steps into leadership roles with ease, guiding his team with authority and inspiring them to follow his lead. Coronamon's leadership skills highlight Leo's role as a natural-born leader.

3. **Creativity and Self-Expression**: Coronamon's creative approach to solving problems and his passionate execution of his missions align with Leo's emphasis on creativity and self-expression. He often finds innovative ways to achieve his goals, reflecting Leo's desire to express themselves creatively. Coronamon's passion and enthusiasm for his missions embody Leo's dynamic and artistic energy.

4. **Generosity and Warmth**: Coronamon's generous nature and warm-hearted demeanor mirror Leo's generosity and warmth. He readily offers his strength and support to his friends, ensuring they feel valued and cared for. Coronamon's willingness to share his power and provide emotional support highlights Leo's generous and loving spirit.

5. **Pride and Honor**: Coronamon's strong sense of pride and honor is a testament to Leo's value of dignity and reputation. He carries himself with dignity and strives to maintain his honor in all his actions. Coronamon's pride in his abilities and his commitment to upholding his values embody Leo's noble and honorable nature.

6. **Loyalty and Protection**: Coronamon's fierce loyalty and protective instincts align with Leo's loyalty and protective nature. He is dedicated to safeguarding Marcus and his companions, demonstrating unwavering loyalty and a strong sense of duty. Coronamon's protective actions and his commitment to his friends reflect Leo's fierce loyalty and protective spirit.

Conclusion

In "Digital Cosmos: The Astrological Digimon Compendium," Coronamon serves as a powerful representation of Leo's qualities of charisma, confidence, and leadership. His character, marked by dynamic energy, courageous spirit, and generous nature, mirrors Leo's influence on our actions, values, and relationships. Through Coronamon's journey, we gain a deeper appreciation for the ways in which the digital and celestial realms intertwine, enriching our understanding of both Digimon and astrology.

As we continue to explore the Digital Cosmos, we will uncover how other Digimon characters embody the traits and energies of different astrological signs and celestial events. Let Coronamon's regal presence and charismatic leadership guide us through this cosmic journey, revealing the profound connections between the worlds of Digimon and astrology.

Chapter 16: Virgo: Renamon's Perfectionist Approach
Characteristics of Virgo in Astrology

Virgo, the sixth sign of the zodiac, is ruled by Mercury and symbolizes practicality, meticulousness, and service. Represented by the virgin, Virgo is associated with the earth element, reflecting its grounded, analytical, and detail-oriented nature. People influenced by Virgo are often seen as perfectionists, highly organized, and dedicated to improving themselves and their surroundings. They value precision, efficiency, and a strong sense of duty.

Key characteristics of Virgo in astrology include:

- **Practicality and Realism**: Virgo is known for its practical approach to life, focusing on realistic and achievable goals.
- **Attention to Detail**: It embodies meticulousness and precision, always paying close attention to the finer details.
- **Analytical and Critical Thinking**: Virgo possesses strong analytical skills, often breaking down complex problems into manageable parts.
- **Service and Helpfulness**: It has a strong sense of duty and is often oriented towards helping and serving others.
- **Organization and Cleanliness**: Virgo values order and cleanliness, striving to maintain a well-organized and tidy environment.
- **Health and Wellness**: It has a keen interest in health and wellness, emphasizing the importance of a balanced and healthy lifestyle.

Renamon's Precision and Analytical Skills

Renamon, the fox-like Digimon, is known for her precision, analytical mind, and calm demeanor. As the partner Digimon of Rika Nonaka in Digimon Tamers, Renamon exhibits traits that align closely with the characteristics of Virgo. Her ability to evolve into powerful forms like

Kyubimon and Sakuyamon highlights her disciplined and methodical nature, making her a formidable and reliable ally.

Key attributes of Renamon's precision and analytical skills include:

- **Precision in Combat**: Renamon's fighting style is marked by precision and efficiency, executing her moves with accuracy and control.
- **Analytical Mind**: She possesses a keen analytical mind, often assessing situations carefully and making strategic decisions.
- **Calm and Composed**: Renamon maintains a calm and composed demeanor, allowing her to stay focused and effective in challenging situations.
- **Discipline and Training**: She is highly disciplined, dedicating herself to rigorous training to improve her skills and abilities.
- **Helpfulness and Support**: Renamon is supportive of Rika and the other Tamers, providing assistance and guidance when needed.
- **Health and Fitness**: She emphasizes the importance of physical fitness and mental discipline, reflecting a focus on health and wellness.

How Renamon Reflects Virgo's Meticulous and Service-Oriented Nature

Renamon's character and actions throughout the Digimon series vividly illustrate Virgo's influence on meticulousness, service, and analytical thinking. Her precise combat skills, analytical mind, and dedication to helping others make her a perfect embodiment of Virgo's qualities.

1. **Practicality and Realism**: Renamon's practical approach to challenges reflects Virgo's focus on realism and achievable goals. She assesses situations logically and develops practical solutions to overcome obstacles. Renamon's grounded nature and her ability

to stay realistic in her strategies embody Virgo's practical mind-set.

2. **Attention to Detail**: Renamon's meticulous attention to detail is evident in her combat style and daily routines. She executes her moves with precision and ensures that every action is carefully calculated. Renamon's focus on the finer details highlights Virgo's emphasis on meticulousness and precision.

3. **Analytical and Critical Thinking**: Renamon's analytical mind and critical thinking skills align with Virgo's strong analytical abilities. She often breaks down complex problems into manageable parts, allowing her to devise effective strategies. Renamon's ability to think critically and analyze situations embodies Virgo's analytical prowess.

4. **Service and Helpfulness**: Renamon's dedication to helping and supporting Rika and the other Tamers reflects Virgo's service-oriented nature. She often puts the needs of others above her own, providing assistance and guidance when needed. Renamon's sense of duty and her commitment to serving others embody Virgo's helpful and service-oriented spirit.

5. **Organization and Cleanliness**: Renamon's disciplined and organized approach to her training and daily activities highlights Virgo's value of order and cleanliness. She maintains a structured routine and strives to keep her environment tidy and efficient. Renamon's organizational skills and her emphasis on maintaining order reflect Virgo's meticulous nature.

6. **Health and Wellness**: Renamon's focus on physical fitness and mental discipline aligns with Virgo's interest in health and wellness. She emphasizes the importance of maintaining a healthy and balanced lifestyle, ensuring that she is always in peak condition. Renamon's commitment to health and wellness embodies Virgo's holistic approach to well-being.

Conclusion

In "Digital Cosmos: The Astrological Digimon Compendium," Renamon serves as a powerful representation of Virgo's qualities of meticulousness, service, and analytical thinking. Her character, marked by precision, discipline, and a strong sense of duty, mirrors Virgo's influence on our actions, values, and relationships. Through Renamon's journey, we gain a deeper appreciation for the ways in which the digital and celestial realms intertwine, enriching our understanding of both Digimon and astrology.

As we continue to explore the Digital Cosmos, we will uncover how other Digimon characters embody the traits and energies of different astrological signs and celestial events. Let Renamon's perfectionist approach and service-oriented nature guide us through this cosmic journey, revealing the profound connections between the worlds of Digimon and astrology.

Chapter 17: Libra: Terriermon's Balanced Harmony
Characteristics of Libra in Astrology

Libra, the seventh sign of the zodiac, is ruled by Venus and symbolizes balance, harmony, and justice. Represented by the scales, Libra is associated with the air element, reflecting its intellectual, diplomatic, and sociable nature. People influenced by Libra are often seen as fair-minded, charming, and keen on maintaining peace and equilibrium in their relationships and environments.

Key characteristics of Libra in astrology include:

- **Balance and Harmony**: Libra values balance and strives for harmony in all aspects of life.
- **Justice and Fairness**: It embodies a strong sense of justice and fairness, always seeking to do what is right.
- **Diplomacy and Mediation**: Libra is skilled in diplomacy, often acting as a mediator to resolve conflicts and maintain peace.
- **Charm and Sociability**: It is naturally charming and sociable, enjoying interactions and forming strong relationships.
- **Intellectual and Analytical**: Libra possesses strong intellectual and analytical skills, often weighing all sides of an issue before making a decision.

- **Aesthetic Appreciation**: Ruled by Venus, Libra has a keen appreciation for beauty, art, and the finer things in life.

Terriermon's Sense of Justice and Balance

Terriermon, the dog-like Digimon, is known for his sense of justice, balanced nature, and playful personality. As the partner Digimon of Henry Wong in Digimon Tamers, Terriermon exhibits traits that align closely with the characteristics of Libra. His ability to evolve into powerful forms like Gargomon and Rapidmon highlights his commitment to justice and his balanced approach to challenges.

Key attributes of Terriermon's sense of justice and balance include:

- **Fairness and Justice**: Terriermon has a strong sense of justice and is committed to doing what is right.
- **Playfulness and Sociability**: He is playful and sociable, often lightening the mood and fostering positive interactions.
- **Diplomacy and Mediation**: Terriermon often acts as a mediator, helping to resolve conflicts and maintain harmony within the group.
- **Calm and Composed**: He maintains a calm and composed demeanor, allowing him to stay balanced and effective in various situations.
- **Intellectual and Strategic**: Terriermon possesses strong analytical skills, often devising strategies to overcome challenges.
- **Adaptability**: He adapts to different situations with ease, showcasing flexibility and resilience.

How Terriermon Embodies Libra's Diplomatic and Fair-Minded Qualities

Terriermon's character and actions throughout the Digimon series vividly illustrate Libra's influence on diplomacy, fairness, and balance. His sense of justice, diplomatic skills, and balanced nature make him a perfect embodiment of Libra's qualities.

1. **Balance and Harmony**: Terriermon's balanced nature and ability to maintain harmony reflect Libra's value of balance and equilibrium. He often acts as a calming influence within the group, helping to keep tensions low and fostering a sense of unity. Terriermon's commitment to maintaining harmony embodies Libra's desire for balanced relationships and environments.

2. **Justice and Fairness**: Terriermon's strong sense of justice and commitment to doing what is right align with Libra's focus on fairness and justice. He often steps in to defend those who are being treated unfairly and works to ensure that everyone is treated with respect. Terriermon's actions highlight Libra's dedication to upholding justice and fairness.

3. **Diplomacy and Mediation**: Terriermon's diplomatic skills and ability to mediate conflicts mirror Libra's talent for diplomacy and mediation. He often acts as a mediator within the group, helping to resolve disputes and maintain peace. Terriermon's diplomatic approach to conflict resolution embodies Libra's role as a peacemaker.

4. **Charm and Sociability**: Terriermon's playful and sociable personality reflects Libra's charm and sociability. He enjoys interacting with others and often uses his charm to foster positive relationships. Terriermon's ability to bring people together and create a positive atmosphere highlights Libra's sociable and charming nature.

5. **Intellectual and Analytical**: Terriermon's strong analytical skills and strategic thinking align with Libra's intellectual and analytical traits. He carefully weighs all sides of an issue before making a decision, ensuring that his actions are fair and well-considered. Terriermon's ability to think critically and devise effective strategies embodies Libra's analytical prowess.

6. **Aesthetic Appreciation**: While not as prominent as other traits, Terriermon's appreciation for beauty and the finer things in life can be seen in his enjoyment of peaceful and harmonious envi-

ronments. His playful nature and love for positive interactions reflect Libra's appreciation for aesthetic and social harmony.

Conclusion

In "Digital Cosmos: The Astrological Digimon Compendium," Terriermon serves as a powerful representation of Libra's qualities of balance, diplomacy, and fairness. His character, marked by a strong sense of justice, diplomatic skills, and a balanced approach to challenges, mirrors Libra's influence on our actions, values, and relationships. Through Terriermon's journey, we gain a deeper appreciation for the ways in which the digital and celestial realms intertwine, enriching our understanding of both Digimon and astrology.

As we continue to explore the Digital Cosmos, we will uncover how other Digimon characters embody the traits and energies of different astrological signs and celestial events. Let Terriermon's balanced harmony and diplomatic nature guide us through this cosmic journey, revealing the profound connections between the worlds of Digimon and astrology.

Chapter 18: Scorpio: Impmon's Intense Transformation
Characteristics of Scorpio in Astrology

Scorpio, the eighth sign of the zodiac, is ruled by Pluto (and traditionally by Mars) and symbolizes transformation, intensity, and mystery. Represented by the scorpion, Scorpio is associated with the water element, reflecting its emotional depth, power, and ability to undergo profound change. People influenced by Scorpio are often seen as passionate, determined, and enigmatic, valuing truth, resilience, and the power of transformation.

Key characteristics of Scorpio in astrology include:

- **Depth and Intensity**: Scorpio experiences emotions and life events with great depth and intensity.
- **Transformation and Rebirth**: It embodies the power of transformation, often undergoing profound personal change.
- **Passion and Determination**: Scorpio is driven by passion and has a relentless determination to achieve its goals.
- **Mystery and Secrecy**: It is known for its enigmatic and secretive nature, often keeping its true thoughts and feelings hidden.
- **Resilience and Strength**: Scorpio possesses incredible resilience and inner strength, capable of overcoming significant challenges.
- **Focus and Resourcefulness**: It is highly focused and resourceful, using its skills and insights to navigate complex situations.

Impmon's Intense and Transformative Journey

Impmon, the mischievous and rebellious Digimon, undergoes one of the most intense and transformative journeys in the Digimon series. Initially driven by a desire for power and recognition, Impmon's path leads him through darkness and despair. However, through his experiences and the realization of the consequences of his actions, he ultimately seeks redemption and transformation into the powerful Beelzemon, and eventually, Beelzemon Blast Mode.

Key aspects of Impmon's intense and transformative journey include:

- **Desire for Power**: Impmon's initial quest for power and recognition leads him to make dark and dangerous choices.
- **Rebellion and Conflict**: His rebellious nature and internal conflicts drive him away from those who care for him, leading to isolation.
- **Realization and Guilt**: Impmon eventually realizes the harm he has caused, experiencing profound guilt and remorse.
- **Quest for Redemption**: Seeking to atone for his past, Impmon embarks on a journey of redemption, striving to protect and aid those he once harmed.
- **Transformation and Rebirth**: His transformation into Beelzemon and later into Beelzemon Blast Mode symbolizes his rebirth and the profound change in his character.
- **Strength and Resilience**: Impmon's journey highlights his inner strength and resilience, demonstrating his ability to overcome significant challenges.

How Impmon Channels Scorpio's Depth, Intensity, and Transformative Power

Impmon's character and actions throughout the Digimon series vividly illustrate Scorpio's influence on depth, intensity, and transformation. His intense emotions, transformative journey, and resilient nature make him a perfect embodiment of Scorpio's qualities.

1. **Depth and Intensity**: Impmon's experiences and emotions are marked by great depth and intensity, reflecting Scorpio's characteristic intensity. His journey is driven by powerful desires and

profound emotional experiences, highlighting the deep and complex nature of his character. Impmon's intense emotional landscape embodies Scorpio's depth and passion.

2. **Transformation and Rebirth**: Impmon's transformation into Beelzemon and later into Beelzemon Blast Mode represents Scorpio's theme of transformation and rebirth. His journey from a mischievous troublemaker to a powerful and redeemed warrior symbolizes the profound change and personal growth that Scorpio governs. Impmon's ability to undergo such significant transformation highlights Scorpio's transformative power.

3. **Passion and Determination**: Impmon's passionate drive for power and his later determination to seek redemption align with Scorpio's intense passion and relentless determination. His actions are fueled by strong desires and an unwavering commitment to his goals, whether they stem from a quest for power or a need for atonement. Impmon's passionate nature and determination embody Scorpio's fierce drive.

4. **Mystery and Secrecy**: Impmon's enigmatic and secretive nature mirrors Scorpio's affinity for mystery and secrecy. He often hides his true thoughts and feelings, presenting a façade that conceals his deeper emotions and struggles. Impmon's mysterious demeanor and the layers of his character reflect Scorpio's secretive and complex nature.

5. **Resilience and Strength**: Impmon's ability to overcome significant challenges and his resilience in the face of adversity are clear manifestations of Scorpio's resilience and inner strength. Despite the darkness he encounters, Impmon finds the strength to transform and redeem himself. His journey highlights the incredible resilience and strength that Scorpio possesses.

6. **Focus and Resourcefulness**: Impmon's strategic thinking and resourcefulness in achieving his goals align with Scorpio's focus and resourcefulness. He navigates complex situations and uses his skills and insights to overcome obstacles. Impmon's focused and

resourceful nature embodies Scorpio's ability to navigate challenges with determination and skill.

Conclusion

In "Digital Cosmos: The Astrological Digimon Compendium," Impmon serves as a powerful representation of Scorpio's qualities of depth, intensity, and transformation. His character, marked by intense emotions, profound transformation, and resilient strength, mirrors Scorpio's influence on our actions, values, and personal growth. Through Impmon's journey, we gain a deeper appreciation for the ways in which the digital and celestial realms intertwine, enriching our understanding of both Digimon and astrology.

As we continue to explore the Digital Cosmos, we will uncover how other Digimon characters embody the traits and energies of different astrological signs and celestial events. Let Impmon's intense transformation and resilient spirit guide us through this cosmic journey, revealing the profound connections between the worlds of Digimon and astrology.

**Chapter 19: Sagittarius: Hawkmon's Adventurous Spirit
Characteristics of Sagittarius in Astrology**

Sagittarius, the ninth sign of the zodiac, is ruled by Jupiter and symbolizes adventure, freedom, and the pursuit of knowledge. Represented by the archer, Sagittarius is associated with the fire element, reflecting its dynamic, optimistic, and enthusiastic nature. People influenced by Sagittarius are often seen as adventurous, philosophical, and eager to explore new horizons, valuing truth, wisdom, and the quest for higher understanding.

Key characteristics of Sagittarius in astrology include:

- **Adventurous and Free-Spirited**: Sagittarius loves adventure and seeks freedom, always eager to explore new places and experiences.
- **Optimism and Enthusiasm**: It embodies a positive and enthusiastic outlook on life, often inspiring others with its energy.
- **Pursuit of Knowledge**: Sagittarius has a strong desire for learning and the pursuit of knowledge, constantly seeking to expand its understanding of the world.
- **Philosophical and Truth-Seeking**: It is deeply philosophical, valuing truth, wisdom, and a higher understanding of life's mysteries.

- **Honesty and Integrity**: Sagittarius values honesty and integrity, often speaking candidly and straightforwardly.
- **Restlessness and Wanderlust**: Its restless nature drives it to constantly seek new experiences and avoid routine and monotony.

Hawkmon's Love for Exploration and Knowledge

Hawkmon, the bird-like Digimon, is known for his adventurous spirit, curiosity, and quest for knowledge. As the partner Digimon of Yolei Inoue in Digimon Adventure 02, Hawkmon exhibits traits that align closely with the characteristics of Sagittarius. His ability to evolve into powerful forms like Aquilamon and Silphymon highlights his dynamic and explorative nature, making him an eager and insightful companion.

Key attributes of Hawkmon's love for exploration and knowledge include:

- **Curiosity and Learning**: Hawkmon has an insatiable curiosity and a love for learning, always seeking to expand his knowledge.
- **Adventurous and Brave**: He is adventurous and brave, often exploring new places and facing challenges with enthusiasm.
- **Honesty and Candor**: Hawkmon values honesty and often speaks candidly, embodying integrity and straightforwardness.
- **Optimism and Enthusiasm**: He maintains an optimistic and enthusiastic attitude, inspiring others with his energy and positive outlook.
- **Philosophical Nature**: Hawkmon possesses a philosophical side, often reflecting on deeper meanings and truths.
- **Restlessness and Wanderlust**: His restless nature drives him to constantly seek new experiences and avoid monotony.

How Hawkmon Embodies Sagittarius's Adventurous and Philosophical Traits

Hawkmon's character and actions throughout the Digimon series vividly illustrate Sagittarius's influence on adventure, knowledge, and philosophy. His adventurous spirit, quest for learning, and optimistic outlook make him a perfect embodiment of Sagittarius's qualities.

1. **Adventurous and Free-Spirited**: Hawkmon's love for adventure and his free-spirited nature reflect Sagittarius's characteristic desire for exploration and freedom. He is always eager to embark on new journeys and discover uncharted territories. Hawkmon's adventurous spirit embodies Sagittarius's quest for new experiences and boundless exploration.

2. **Optimism and Enthusiasm**: Hawkmon's optimistic and enthusiastic attitude aligns with Sagittarius's positive outlook on life. He approaches challenges with energy and enthusiasm, often inspiring his friends with his upbeat demeanor. Hawkmon's ability to maintain a positive attitude in various situations highlights Sagittarius's innate optimism.

3. **Pursuit of Knowledge**: Hawkmon's insatiable curiosity and love for learning mirror Sagittarius's pursuit of knowledge. He is constantly seeking to expand his understanding of the world and acquire new insights. Hawkmon's quest for knowledge and his eagerness to learn embody Sagittarius's intellectual curiosity and desire for wisdom.

4. **Philosophical and Truth-Seeking**: Hawkmon's philosophical nature and his reflections on deeper meanings align with Sagittarius's truth-seeking and philosophical traits. He often contemplates the greater purpose and underlying truths of his experiences, showcasing a thoughtful and reflective side. Hawkmon's philosophical approach to life highlights Sagittarius's quest for higher understanding and truth.

5. **Honesty and Integrity**: Hawkmon's value of honesty and his straightforward communication reflect Sagittarius's emphasis on integrity and candor. He often speaks candidly and truthfully, embodying the principles of honesty and integrity. Hawkmon's forthrightness and commitment to truth highlight Sagittarius's ethical and sincere nature.

6. **Restlessness and Wanderlust**: Hawkmon's restless nature and desire for constant movement and new experiences align with Sagittarius's wanderlust. He dislikes routine and monotony, always seeking fresh adventures and challenges. Hawkmon's restless energy and his drive to explore new horizons embody Sagittarius's dynamic and exploratory spirit.

Conclusion

In "Digital Cosmos: The Astrological Digimon Compendium," Hawkmon serves as a powerful representation of Sagittarius's qualities of adventure, knowledge, and philosophical insight. His character, marked by an adventurous spirit, insatiable curiosity, and optimistic outlook, mirrors Sagittarius's influence on our actions, values, and quest for understanding. Through Hawkmon's journey, we gain a deeper appreciation for the ways in which the digital and celestial realms intertwine, enriching our understanding of both Digimon and astrology.

As we continue to explore the Digital Cosmos, we will uncover how other Digimon characters embody the traits and energies of different astrological signs and celestial events. Let Hawkmon's adventurous spirit and philosophical nature guide us through this cosmic journey, revealing the profound connections between the worlds of Digimon and astrology.

Chapter 20: Capricorn: Armadillomon's Steadfast Persistence
Characteristics of Capricorn in Astrology

Capricorn, the tenth sign of the zodiac, is ruled by Saturn and symbolizes discipline, responsibility, and ambition. Represented by the mountain goat, Capricorn is associated with the earth element, reflecting its grounded, practical, and determined nature. People influenced by Capricorn are often seen as hardworking, persistent, and goal-oriented, valuing achievement, structure, and long-term success.

Key characteristics of Capricorn in astrology include:

- **Discipline and Responsibility**: Capricorn embodies discipline, a strong sense of duty, and a responsible approach to life.
- **Ambition and Goal-Oriented**: It is highly ambitious, setting high standards and working diligently to achieve its goals.
- **Practicality and Realism**: Capricorn has a practical and realistic outlook, focusing on tangible results and concrete achievements.
- **Persistence and Determination**: It is known for its steadfast persistence and determination, never giving up in the face of obstacles.
- **Patience and Endurance**: Capricorn values patience and endurance, understanding that success often requires sustained effort over time.
- **Structure and Order**: It values structure, organization, and a methodical approach to tasks.

Armadillomon's Hardworking and Persistent Nature

Armadillomon, the armadillo-like Digimon, is known for his hardworking, persistent, and steadfast nature. As the partner Digimon of Cody Hida in Digimon Adventure 02, Armadillomon exhibits traits that align closely with the characteristics of Capricorn. His ability to evolve into powerful forms like Digmon and Submarimon highlights his resilience and determination, making him a reliable and steadfast companion.

Key attributes of Armadillomon's hardworking and persistent nature include:

- **Hardworking and Diligent**: Armadillomon is dedicated and hardworking, always putting in the effort required to accomplish tasks.
- **Persistent and Determined**: He demonstrates unwavering persistence and determination, never giving up even when faced with challenges.
- **Reliable and Dependable**: Armadillomon is a reliable and dependable partner, consistently supporting Cody and the other DigiDestined.
- **Practical and Grounded**: He approaches problems with a practical and realistic mindset, finding effective and efficient solutions.
- **Patience and Endurance**: Armadillomon exhibits patience and endurance, understanding that success often requires sustained effort over time.
- **Structured and Methodical**: He values structure and takes a methodical approach to tasks, ensuring that they are completed thoroughly and efficiently.

How Armadillomon Reflects Capricorn's Discipline and Ambition

Armadillomon's character and actions throughout the Digimon series vividly illustrate Capricorn's influence on discipline, responsibility, and ambition. His hardworking demeanor, persistent nature, and practical approach make him a perfect embodiment of Capricorn's qualities.

1. **Discipline and Responsibility**: Armadillomon's disciplined approach to his duties and his strong sense of responsibility re-

flect Capricorn's values. He consistently fulfills his responsibilities and takes his role seriously, demonstrating a disciplined and responsible attitude. Armadillomon's commitment to his duties embodies Capricorn's sense of duty and discipline.

2. **Ambition and Goal-Oriented**: Armadillomon's ambition and focus on achieving his goals align with Capricorn's goal-oriented nature. He sets high standards for himself and works diligently to meet them, always striving for success. Armadillomon's ambitious drive and his pursuit of excellence highlight Capricorn's ambition and determination.

3. **Practicality and Realism**: Armadillomon's practical and realistic approach to challenges mirrors Capricorn's practicality and realism. He assesses situations logically and develops effective solutions, ensuring that his actions are grounded and achievable. Armadillomon's pragmatic mindset and his focus on tangible results embody Capricorn's practical nature.

4. **Persistence and Determination**: Armadillomon's steadfast persistence and determination are clear manifestations of Capricorn's influence. He never gives up, no matter how difficult the task, and continues to push forward with unwavering resolve. Armadillomon's ability to persevere through obstacles and achieve his goals highlights Capricorn's persistent and determined spirit.

5. **Patience and Endurance**: Armadillomon's patience and endurance align with Capricorn's understanding that success often requires sustained effort over time. He approaches tasks with patience and is willing to put in the necessary time and effort to achieve long-term success. Armadillomon's endurance and his ability to stay focused on his goals reflect Capricorn's patient and enduring nature.

6. **Structure and Order**: Armadillomon's structured and methodical approach to tasks highlights Capricorn's value of structure and order. He ensures that tasks are completed thoroughly and efficiently, following a clear and organized plan. Armadillomon's

methodical nature and his emphasis on order and organization embody Capricorn's structured and disciplined approach.

Conclusion

In "Digital Cosmos: The Astrological Digimon Compendium," Armadillomon serves as a powerful representation of Capricorn's qualities of discipline, responsibility, and ambition. His character, marked by hardworking diligence, persistent determination, and a practical approach to challenges, mirrors Capricorn's influence on our actions, values, and pursuit of long-term success. Through Armadillomon's journey, we gain a deeper appreciation for the ways in which the digital and celestial realms intertwine, enriching our understanding of both Digimon and astrology.

As we continue to explore the Digital Cosmos, we will uncover how other Digimon characters embody the traits and energies of different astrological signs and celestial events. Let Armadillomon's steadfast persistence and disciplined nature guide us through this cosmic journey, revealing the profound connections between the worlds of Digimon and astrology.

Chapter 21: Aquarius: Betamon's Innovative Thinking

Characteristics of Aquarius in Astrology

Aquarius, the eleventh sign of the zodiac, is ruled by Uranus (and traditionally by Saturn) and symbolizes innovation, independence, and humanitarianism. Represented by the water-bearer, Aquarius is associated with the air element, reflecting its intellectual, forward-thinking, and unconventional nature. People influenced by Aquarius are often seen as visionary, innovative, and socially conscious, valuing progress, equality, and the betterment of humanity.

Key characteristics of Aquarius in astrology include:

- **Innovation and Originality**: Aquarius is known for its innovative and original ideas, often thinking outside the box.
- **Independence and Individuality**: It values independence and individuality, encouraging uniqueness and self-expression.
- **Humanitarianism and Social Awareness**: Aquarius is deeply concerned with social issues and the welfare of humanity, often advocating for equality and justice.
- **Intellectual and Analytical**: It possesses strong intellectual and analytical skills, enjoying abstract thinking and problem-solving.
- **Progressive and Forward-Thinking**: Aquarius is forward-thinking and progressive, always looking towards the future and seeking to improve the world.
- **Unconventional and Eccentric**: It embraces the unconventional and eccentric, often challenging societal norms and embracing new ways of thinking.

Betamon's Uniqueness and Innovative Ideas

Betamon, the amphibious Digimon, is known for his uniqueness, innovative thinking, and adaptability. As the partner Digimon of Michael in Digimon Adventure 02, Betamon exhibits traits that align closely with the characteristics of Aquarius. His ability to evolve into powerful forms like Seadramon and MegaSeadramon highlights his progressive nature and innovative approach to challenges, making him a unique and forward-thinking companion.

Key attributes of Betamon's uniqueness and innovative ideas include:

- **Innovative Thinking**: Betamon often comes up with creative and original solutions to problems, thinking outside the box.
- **Independence and Uniqueness**: He values his independence and embraces his unique abilities and characteristics.
- **Social Awareness and Compassion**: Betamon shows a strong sense of social awareness and compassion, often helping those in need and advocating for justice.
- **Adaptability**: He is highly adaptable, able to thrive in various environments and situations.
- **Analytical Skills**: Betamon possesses strong analytical skills, often assessing situations carefully and devising effective strategies.
- **Progressive and Forward-Thinking**: He is always looking towards the future, seeking to improve and evolve in innovative ways.

How Betamon Channels Aquarius's Progressive and Humanitarian Energy

Betamon's character and actions throughout the Digimon series vividly illustrate Aquarius's influence on innovation, humanitarianism, and progressive thinking. His unique abilities, innovative ideas, and social consciousness make him a perfect embodiment of Aquarius's qualities.

1. **Innovation and Originality**: Betamon's ability to come up with creative and original solutions to problems reflects Aquarius's characteristic innovation and originality. He often thinks

outside the box and devises unique strategies to overcome challenges. Betamon's innovative thinking embodies Aquarius's desire to push boundaries and explore new possibilities.

2. **Independence and Individuality**: Betamon's independent nature and embrace of his unique abilities align with Aquarius's value of independence and individuality. He is confident in his distinct characteristics and often relies on his unique skills to navigate challenges. Betamon's individuality and self-expression highlight Aquarius's encouragement of uniqueness and personal freedom.

3. **Humanitarianism and Social Awareness**: Betamon's strong sense of social awareness and compassion mirrors Aquarius's concern for social issues and humanitarianism. He often helps those in need and advocates for fairness and justice. Betamon's actions to support and protect others embody Aquarius's dedication to the welfare of humanity and social equality.

4. **Intellectual and Analytical**: Betamon's strong analytical skills and intellectual approach to problem-solving align with Aquarius's intellectual and analytical traits. He carefully assesses situations and develops well-thought-out strategies to achieve his goals. Betamon's analytical mind and problem-solving abilities reflect Aquarius's intellectual prowess.

5. **Progressive and Forward-Thinking**: Betamon's progressive nature and forward-thinking approach to challenges mirror Aquarius's desire for progress and future-oriented thinking. He is always looking for ways to improve and evolve, seeking innovative solutions to enhance his capabilities. Betamon's forward-thinking attitude highlights Aquarius's commitment to progress and improvement.

6. **Unconventional and Eccentric**: Betamon's embrace of the unconventional and his willingness to challenge norms align with Aquarius's acceptance of eccentricity and unconventional thinking. He often takes unconventional approaches to problems,

demonstrating a willingness to explore new and unorthodox methods. Betamon's unconventional nature and innovative ideas embody Aquarius's embrace of new and radical perspectives.

Conclusion

In "Digital Cosmos: The Astrological Digimon Compendium," Betamon serves as a powerful representation of Aquarius's qualities of innovation, humanitarianism, and progressive thinking. His character, marked by unique abilities, innovative ideas, and social consciousness, mirrors Aquarius's influence on our actions, values, and pursuit of a better world. Through Betamon's journey, we gain a deeper appreciation for the ways in which the digital and celestial realms intertwine, enriching our understanding of both Digimon and astrology.

As we continue to explore the Digital Cosmos, we will uncover how other Digimon characters embody the traits and energies of different astrological signs and celestial events. Let Betamon's innovative thinking and humanitarian spirit guide us through this cosmic journey, revealing the profound connections between the worlds of Digimon and astrology.

Chapter 22: Pisces: Elecmon's Compassionate Understanding Characteristics of Pisces in Astrology

Pisces, the twelfth and final sign of the zodiac, is ruled by Neptune (and traditionally by Jupiter) and symbolizes empathy, intuition, and the mystical. Represented by two fish swimming in opposite directions, Pisces is associated with the water element, reflecting its emotional depth, sensitivity, and fluidity. People influenced by Pisces are often seen as compassionate, imaginative, and spiritually inclined, valuing connection, empathy, and the mysteries of life.

Key characteristics of Pisces in astrology include:

- **Empathy and Compassion**: Pisces is deeply empathetic and compassionate, often feeling the emotions of others as their own.
- **Intuition and Psychic Abilities**: It possesses strong intuitive and psychic abilities, often having a deep understanding of unseen realms.
- **Mystical and Spiritual**: Pisces is drawn to the mystical and spiritual, seeking to connect with the divine and explore the mysteries of existence.
- **Imagination and Creativity**: It is highly imaginative and creative, often finding expression through art, music, and other creative endeavors.
- **Sensitivity and Emotional Depth**: Pisces experiences emotions with great depth and sensitivity, often being deeply moved by the world around them.
- **Adaptability and Fluidity**: It is adaptable and fluid, able to navigate various situations with ease and grace.

Elecmon's Empathy and Mystical Qualities

Elecmon, the electric Digimon, is known for his empathy, gentle nature, and mystical qualities. As the caretaker of the Baby Digimon in Primary Village, Elecmon exhibits traits that align closely with the characteristics of Pisces. His role as a nurturer and protector highlights his deep compassion and intuitive understanding, making him a wise and gentle guardian.

Key attributes of Elecmon's empathy and mystical qualities include:

- **Empathy and Compassion**: Elecmon shows deep empathy and compassion, caring for the Baby Digimon with great tenderness and understanding.
- **Intuitive Understanding**: He possesses a strong intuitive sense, often understanding the needs and emotions of the Baby Digimon instinctively.
- **Nurturing and Protective**: Elecmon is a dedicated caretaker, nurturing and protecting the young Digimon with unwavering dedication.
- **Mystical and Spiritual**: He exhibits a mystical and spiritual presence, often conveying a sense of wisdom and connection to the greater mysteries of the Digital World.
- **Creativity and Imagination**: Elecmon's approach to caring for the Baby Digimon is marked by creativity and imagination, finding unique ways to nurture and entertain them.
- **Sensitivity and Emotional Depth**: He experiences emotions with great depth and sensitivity, often being deeply moved by the experiences of the Baby Digimon.

How Elecmon Embodies Pisces's Intuitive and Compassionate Traits

Elecmon's character and actions throughout the Digimon series vividly illustrate Pisces's influence on empathy, intuition, and mystical understanding. His compassionate nature, intuitive abilities, and mystical presence make him a perfect embodiment of Pisces's qualities.

1. **Empathy and Compassion**: Elecmon's deep empathy and compassion reflect Pisces's characteristic sensitivity and caring nature.

He cares for the Baby Digimon with great tenderness, often understanding their needs and emotions intuitively. Elecmon's ability to connect with and nurture the young Digimon embodies Pisces's compassionate spirit.

2. **Intuition and Psychic Abilities**: Elecmon's strong intuitive sense aligns with Pisces's emphasis on intuition and psychic abilities. He often knows what the Baby Digimon need without being told, relying on his intuitive understanding to guide his actions. Elecmon's instinctive care and guidance highlight Pisces's intuitive and psychic traits.

3. **Mystical and Spiritual**: Elecmon's mystical and spiritual presence mirrors Pisces's attraction to the mystical and spiritual realms. He conveys a sense of wisdom and connection to the greater mysteries of the Digital World, often guiding the Baby Digimon with a calm and serene demeanor. Elecmon's spiritual nature embodies Pisces's quest for deeper understanding and connection.

4. **Imagination and Creativity**: Elecmon's creative approach to nurturing the Baby Digimon reflects Pisces's imaginative and creative qualities. He finds unique and inventive ways to care for and entertain them, ensuring their well-being and happiness. Elecmon's creativity and imaginative spirit highlight Pisces's artistic and expressive nature.

5. **Sensitivity and Emotional Depth**: Elecmon's sensitivity and emotional depth align with Pisces's characteristic emotional intensity. He experiences and responds to the emotions of the Baby Digimon with great depth, often being deeply moved by their experiences. Elecmon's emotional sensitivity and his ability to provide comfort and support embody Pisces's empathetic and compassionate traits.

6. **Adaptability and Fluidity**: Elecmon's adaptability and fluid approach to caring for the Baby Digimon reflect Pisces's fluid and adaptable nature. He navigates various situations with ease and

grace, adjusting his care to meet the changing needs of the young Digimon. Elecmon's flexibility and adaptability highlight Pisces's ability to go with the flow and respond to the needs of the moment.

Conclusion

In "Digital Cosmos: The Astrological Digimon Compendium," Elecmon serves as a powerful representation of Pisces's qualities of empathy, intuition, and mystical understanding. His character, marked by deep compassion, intuitive abilities, and a nurturing spirit, mirrors Pisces's influence on our actions, values, and connections to the mystical realms. Through Elecmon's journey, we gain a deeper appreciation for the ways in which the digital and celestial realms intertwine, enriching our understanding of both Digimon and astrology.

As we conclude our exploration of the Digital Cosmos, we have uncovered how various Digimon characters embody the traits and energies of different astrological signs and celestial events. Let Elecmon's compassionate understanding and intuitive nature remind us of the profound connections between the worlds of Digimon and astrology, and inspire us to embrace these qualities in our own lives.

Part 3: Celestial Bodies and Digital Alignments

Chapter 23: The North Node: Guiding Destinies with Angemon

Characteristics of the North Node in Astrology

In astrology, the North Node represents our karmic path and the lessons we need to learn in this lifetime. It points towards our true purpose, guiding us toward growth and fulfillment. Unlike the planets, the North Node is a mathematical point created by the intersection of the moon's orbit with the ecliptic. It symbolizes the future and the direction in which we are meant to evolve, often presenting challenges that push us out of our comfort zones and into our highest potential.

Key characteristics of the North Node in astrology include:

- **Destiny and Purpose**: The North Node represents our life's purpose and the direction we are meant to follow to fulfill our destiny.
- **Spiritual Growth**: It encourages spiritual growth and evolution, guiding us to overcome past limitations and embrace our true potential.
- **Karmic Lessons**: The North Node highlights the karmic lessons we need to learn in this lifetime to progress on our spiritual journey.
- **Challenges and Growth**: It often presents challenges and obstacles that push us to grow and evolve beyond our comfort zones.
- **Future-Oriented**: The North Node is future-oriented, focusing on where we are going rather than where we have been.
- **Transformation**: It signifies profound personal transformation, leading us towards a more authentic and fulfilling life path.

Angemon's Role as a Guide and Protector

Angemon, the angelic Digimon, is known for his role as a guide and protector. As the Digivolved form of Patamon, Angemon plays a crucial role in supporting the DigiDestined, particularly T.K. Takaishi. His presence symbolizes hope, righteousness, and the fight against evil. Angemon's ability to evolve into MagnaAngemon further enhances his role as a powerful guide and protector, embodying the qualities of a guardian angel.

Key attributes of Angemon's role as a guide and protector include:

- **Guidance and Wisdom**: Angemon provides guidance and wisdom to the DigiDestined, helping them navigate their challenges and fulfill their destinies.
- **Protection**: He is a fierce protector, defending his friends from the forces of darkness and ensuring their safety.
- **Righteousness**: Angemon embodies righteousness and justice, always striving to do what is right and just.
- **Spiritual Strength**: His angelic nature symbolizes spiritual strength and the power of light over darkness.
- **Hope and Inspiration**: Angemon inspires hope and courage in the DigiDestined, encouraging them to persevere in the face of adversity.
- **Transformation**: His evolution from Patamon to Angemon, and eventually to MagnaAngemon, signifies profound personal transformation and growth.

How Angemon Represents the North Node's Influence on Destiny and Spiritual Growth

Angemon's character and actions throughout the Digimon series vividly illustrate the North Node's influence on destiny, spiritual growth, and personal transformation. His role as a guide and protector, coupled with his righteous nature, makes him a perfect embodiment of the North Node's qualities.

1. **Destiny and Purpose**: Angemon's guidance helps the DigiDestined, especially T.K., to understand and fulfill their destinies.

His presence in their lives directs them towards their true purpose, embodying the North Node's role in guiding us towards our life's mission. Angemon's influence ensures that the DigiDestined stay on their path, fulfilling their roles in the Digital World's balance.

2. **Spiritual Growth**: Angemon's angelic nature and his ability to inspire spiritual strength in others align with the North Node's emphasis on spiritual growth. He encourages the DigiDestined to rise above their fears and doubts, fostering their spiritual evolution. Angemon's role in guiding them through their challenges highlights the North Node's influence on our spiritual journey.

3. **Karmic Lessons**: Angemon's presence often comes at pivotal moments when the DigiDestined face significant challenges and karmic lessons. His guidance helps them to learn and grow from these experiences, embodying the North Node's role in teaching us the lessons we need to progress. Angemon's support during these critical times ensures that the DigiDestined overcome their past limitations and embrace their true potential.

4. **Challenges and Growth**: Angemon's battles against the forces of darkness represent the challenges that the North Node presents to push us out of our comfort zones. Through these battles, the DigiDestined grow stronger and more resilient, embodying the North Node's influence on personal growth and transformation. Angemon's ability to confront and overcome evil highlights the transformative power of facing and overcoming challenges.

5. **Future-Oriented**: Angemon's guidance is always focused on the future and the greater good, aligning with the North Node's future-oriented nature. He helps the DigiDestined to look beyond their immediate struggles and focus on their ultimate goals and destiny. Angemon's forward-thinking approach ensures that they remain focused on their path to fulfilling their destinies.

6. **Transformation**: Angemon's evolution from Patamon to Angemon, and eventually to MagnaAngemon, symbolizes profound

personal transformation. This mirrors the North Node's role in guiding us towards our highest potential and leading us through significant changes that align us with our true purpose. Angemon's transformative journey embodies the North Node's influence on our personal evolution.

Conclusion

In "Digital Cosmos: The Astrological Digimon Compendium," Angemon serves as a powerful representation of the North Node's qualities of destiny, spiritual growth, and personal transformation. His character, marked by guidance, protection, and righteousness, mirrors the North Node's influence on our actions, values, and spiritual journey. Through Angemon's role, we gain a deeper appreciation for the ways in which the digital and celestial realms intertwine, enriching our understanding of both Digimon and astrology.

As we continue to explore the Digital Cosmos, we recognize how various Digimon characters embody the traits and energies of different astrological signs and celestial events. Let Angemon's guiding presence and spiritual strength illuminate our path, revealing the profound connections between the worlds of Digimon and astrology, and inspiring us to embrace our own destinies and spiritual growth.

Chapter 24: The South Node: Learning from the Past with Devimon

Characteristics of the South Node in Astrology

In astrology, the South Node represents our past lives, inherited traits, and the lessons we've already mastered. It symbolizes where we come from and the familiar patterns that we tend to fall back on. Unlike the North Node, which points towards our future growth and purpose, the South Node highlights our past experiences and the qualities we need to balance and integrate to move forward.

Key characteristics of the South Node in astrology include:

- **Past Lives and Karma**: The South Node is associated with past life experiences and the karmic baggage we bring into this lifetime.
- **Comfort Zones**: It represents familiar patterns and behaviors that we are comfortable with but need to evolve from.
- **Mastered Skills**: The South Node highlights the skills and abilities we have already developed and mastered in past experiences.
- **Lessons and Challenges**: It points to the lessons and challenges we have faced, providing a foundation for future growth.
- **Balance and Integration**: The South Node teaches us to balance our past experiences with our future goals, integrating what we have learned into our current life path.
- **Release and Growth**: It encourages us to release outdated patterns and behaviors that no longer serve our growth and evolution.

Devimon's Representation of Past Challenges and Karmic Lessons

Devimon, the dark and malevolent Digimon, is a significant antagonist in the Digimon series. As a representation of the forces of darkness, Devimon embodies past challenges and karmic lessons that the DigiDestined must confront and overcome. His role as a formidable adversary highlights the importance of facing and integrating past influences to move forward.

Key aspects of Devimon's representation of past challenges and karmic lessons include:

- **Darkness and Temptation**: Devimon embodies the darkness and temptation that the DigiDestined must resist and overcome.
- **Challenges and Adversity**: He presents significant challenges and obstacles, forcing the DigiDestined to confront their fears and doubts.
- **Lessons of Strength and Unity**: The battles against Devimon teach the DigiDestined important lessons about strength, unity, and resilience.
- **Karmic Confrontation**: Devimon's presence represents the karmic confrontations the DigiDestined must face to resolve past issues and grow.
- **Transformation through Adversity**: The struggles against Devimon lead to personal transformation and growth for the DigiDestined, highlighting the transformative power of overcoming past challenges.

How Devimon Embodies the South Node's Themes of Past Influences and Lessons

Devimon's character and actions throughout the Digimon series vividly illustrate the South Node's influence on past experiences, karmic lessons, and the need for balance and integration. His role as an antagonist who embodies darkness and past challenges makes him a perfect representation of the South Node's qualities.

1. **Past Lives and Karma**: Devimon's dark and malevolent nature reflects the karmic baggage and past life influences that the DigiDestined must confront. His presence forces them to face unresolved issues from their past, embodying the South Node's connection to past lives and karma. Devimon's role as a dark force highlights the importance of addressing and resolving past influences.

2. **Comfort Zones**: Devimon represents the familiar patterns of fear and temptation that the DigiDestined must overcome. His influence challenges them to move beyond their comfort zones and face their deepest fears. Devimon's presence forces the DigiDestined to break free from familiar but limiting behaviors, embodying the South Node's role in pushing us out of our comfort zones.

3. **Mastered Skills**: The battles against Devimon highlight the skills and abilities the DigiDestined have already developed. They must rely on their strengths and previously learned lessons to confront and overcome Devimon's challenges. Devimon's role emphasizes the importance of utilizing mastered skills to navigate current challenges, reflecting the South Node's focus on past experiences.

4. **Lessons and Challenges**: Devimon presents significant lessons and challenges that the DigiDestined must face to grow and evolve. His presence forces them to confront their fears, doubts, and insecurities, teaching them important lessons about resilience, strength, and unity. Devimon's role as an adversary embodies the South Node's emphasis on learning from past challenges.

5. **Balance and Integration**: The struggles against Devimon highlight the need for the DigiDestined to balance and integrate their past experiences with their current goals. They must learn to use

their past lessons to navigate present challenges, embodying the South Node's focus on balance and integration. Devimon's influence forces the DigiDestined to reconcile their past with their future.

6. **Release and Growth**: Overcoming Devimon requires the DigiDestined to release outdated patterns and behaviors that no longer serve their growth. They must let go of their fears and embrace their true potential, reflecting the South Node's role in encouraging release and growth. Devimon's role as an antagonist highlights the transformative power of releasing past influences to achieve personal growth.

Conclusion

In "Digital Cosmos: The Astrological Digimon Compendium," Devimon serves as a powerful representation of the South Node's qualities of past influences, karmic lessons, and the need for balance and integration. His character, marked by darkness, challenges, and the embodiment of past experiences, mirrors the South Node's influence on our actions, values, and personal growth. Through Devimon's role, we gain a deeper appreciation for the ways in which the digital and celestial realms intertwine, enriching our understanding of both Digimon and astrology.

As we conclude our exploration of the Digital Cosmos, we recognize how various Digimon characters embody the traits and energies of different astrological signs and celestial events. Let Devimon's representation of past challenges and karmic lessons remind us of the importance of integrating our past experiences, learning from them, and moving forward on our path to growth and fulfillment.

**Chapter 25: Chiron: Healing Wounds with Leomon
Characteristics of Chiron in Astrology**

In astrology, Chiron is known as the "Wounded Healer." It represents our deepest wounds and our capacity to heal them, as well as to help others heal. Chiron embodies the paradox of suffering and healing: it highlights the areas of our lives where we feel the most pain and vulnerability, yet also where we possess the greatest potential for healing and wisdom. Chiron's influence encourages us to confront and heal our wounds, turning pain into strength and wisdom.

Key characteristics of Chiron in astrology include:

- **Wounds and Healing**: Chiron represents our deepest emotional, physical, and spiritual wounds, as well as our ability to heal them.
- **Wisdom through Pain**: It embodies the wisdom gained from experiencing and overcoming pain and suffering.
- **Mentorship and Teaching**: Chiron encourages us to use our experiences to mentor and teach others, guiding them through their healing journeys.
- **Empathy and Compassion**: It fosters deep empathy and compassion for others' suffering, enhancing our ability to offer support and understanding.
- **Transformation and Growth**: Chiron's influence leads to profound personal transformation and growth through the process of healing.
- **Vulnerability and Strength**: It highlights the strength found in vulnerability, encouraging us to embrace and address our weaknesses.

Leomon's Role as a Healer and Mentor

Leomon, the lion-like Digimon, is renowned for his wisdom, strength, and noble leadership. As a seasoned warrior and mentor, Leomon plays a crucial role in guiding and protecting the DigiDestined. His character embodies the qualities of a healer and mentor, offering support, wisdom, and strength to those around him. Leomon's journey is marked by profound challenges and sacrifices, highlighting his role as a wounded healer who channels his experiences into guidance and protection for others.

Key attributes of Leomon's role as a healer and mentor include:

- **Wisdom and Guidance**: Leomon provides valuable wisdom and guidance to the DigiDestined, helping them navigate their challenges and grow.
- **Protectiveness and Strength**: He is a fierce protector, using his strength to defend and support his allies.
- **Empathy and Understanding**: Leomon shows deep empathy and understanding, often providing comfort and reassurance to those in need.
- **Mentorship and Teaching**: He takes on the role of a mentor, teaching the DigiDestined important lessons about courage, honor, and resilience.
- **Sacrifice and Healing**: Leomon's sacrifices and healing abilities highlight his role as a wounded healer, transforming his pain into strength and support for others.
- **Noble Leadership**: His noble and honorable nature makes him a respected leader and a source of inspiration for the DigiDestined.

How Leomon Channels Chiron's Energy of Healing and Wisdom through Pain

Leomon's character and actions throughout the Digimon series vividly illustrate Chiron's influence on healing, wisdom, and transformation through pain. His role as a mentor and protector, coupled with his experiences of suffering and sacrifice, make him a perfect embodiment of Chiron's qualities.

1. **Wounds and Healing**: Leomon's journey is marked by significant wounds and healing, reflecting Chiron's role as the Wounded Healer. His battles and sacrifices often result in physical and emotional wounds, yet he continuously heals and grows stronger. Leomon's resilience and ability to heal from his wounds embody Chiron's influence on our capacity to overcome and heal our deepest injuries.

2. **Wisdom through Pain**: Leomon's wisdom and guidance are deeply rooted in his experiences of pain and suffering. He uses his past challenges to offer valuable insights and support to the DigiDestined, helping them navigate their own difficulties. Leomon's ability to transform his pain into wisdom highlights Chiron's theme of gaining profound understanding through suffering.

3. **Mentorship and Teaching**: As a mentor and teacher, Leomon channels Chiron's energy by guiding the DigiDestined through their journeys. He imparts important lessons about courage, honor, and resilience, using his own experiences to mentor and support them. Leomon's role as a mentor reflects Chiron's influence on teaching and guiding others through their healing processes.

4. **Empathy and Compassion**: Leomon's deep empathy and compassion for others' suffering align with Chiron's emphasis on empathy. He provides comfort and reassurance to the DigiDestined, understanding their struggles and offering support. Leomon's compassionate nature and his ability to connect with others' pain embody Chiron's empathetic and supportive qualities.

5. **Transformation and Growth**: Leomon's personal transformation and growth through his experiences of pain and sacrifice mirror Chiron's influence on transformation. His journey from a

powerful warrior to a wise mentor highlights the transformative power of healing and growth through adversity. Leomon's evolution and his ability to turn suffering into strength reflect Chiron's transformative energy.

6. **Vulnerability and Strength**: Leomon's willingness to embrace his vulnerabilities and use them to strengthen and protect others embodies Chiron's theme of finding strength in vulnerability. His sacrifices and struggles make him stronger and more resilient, allowing him to offer greater support to the DigiDestined. Leomon's balance of vulnerability and strength highlights Chiron's influence on embracing and addressing our weaknesses.

Conclusion

In "Digital Cosmos: The Astrological Digimon Compendium," Leomon serves as a powerful representation of Chiron's qualities of healing, wisdom, and transformation through pain. His character, marked by wisdom, empathy, and the ability to turn suffering into strength, mirrors Chiron's influence on our actions, values, and personal growth. Through Leomon's journey, we gain a deeper appreciation for the ways in which the digital and celestial realms intertwine, enriching our understanding of both Digimon and astrology.

As we conclude our exploration of the Digital Cosmos, we recognize how various Digimon characters embody the traits and energies of different astrological signs and celestial events. Let Leomon's healing presence and wise mentorship inspire us to embrace our own wounds, transform our pain into wisdom, and guide others on their journeys, revealing the profound connections between the worlds of Digimon and astrology.

Chapter 26: Lilith: Embracing Shadows with LadyDevimon

Characteristics of Lilith in Astrology

In astrology, Lilith, often referred to as the "Black Moon Lilith," represents the dark, hidden aspects of the psyche and the primal, untamed parts of the self. Lilith embodies the shadow self, the parts of our personality that we repress or deny. She is associated with themes of power, independence, and the embrace of our darker, more taboo desires. Lilith's influence encourages us to confront and integrate these hidden aspects, allowing for a more complete and authentic self.

Key characteristics of Lilith in astrology include:

- **Shadow Self**: Lilith represents the shadow self, encompassing repressed desires, fears, and aspects of the personality that are often hidden.
- **Power and Independence**: She embodies themes of personal power, autonomy, and the rejection of societal norms and restrictions.
- **Taboo and Forbidden**: Lilith is associated with the taboo, the forbidden, and the aspects of ourselves that are considered socially unacceptable.
- **Confrontation and Integration**: Her influence encourages the confrontation and integration of the shadow self, promoting personal growth and self-acceptance.
- **Primal and Instinctual**: Lilith connects us to our primal, instinctual nature, emphasizing raw emotions and desires.
- **Mystery and Seduction**: She has a mysterious and seductive quality, often challenging conventional morality and societal expectations.

LadyDevimon's Connection to Shadow Work and Hidden Aspects

LadyDevimon, the dark and powerful Digimon, is known for her connection to shadow work and the hidden aspects of the self. As a formidable antagonist in the Digimon series, LadyDevimon embodies the qualities of Lilith, representing the darker, repressed parts of the psyche. Her presence and actions challenge the DigiDestined to confront their fears and hidden desires, making her a powerful symbol of Lilith's energy.

Key attributes of LadyDevimon's connection to shadow work and hidden aspects include:

- **Embracing Darkness**: LadyDevimon fully embraces her dark nature, wielding her power without fear or hesitation.
- **Challenge and Confrontation**: She challenges the DigiDestined to confront their inner fears and hidden aspects, pushing them to acknowledge and integrate their shadow selves.
- **Seduction and Mystery**: LadyDevimon's seductive and mysterious presence embodies the allure of the forbidden and the unknown.
- **Power and Autonomy**: She represents personal power and independence, rejecting societal norms and expectations.
- **Fear and Fascination**: Her dark allure evokes both fear and fascination, compelling the DigiDestined to face the darker parts of themselves.
- **Transformation through Darkness**: LadyDevimon's influence leads to transformation and growth through the confrontation of darkness and the integration of the shadow self.

How LadyDevimon Represents Lilith's Themes of Embracing and Integrating the Shadow Self

LadyDevimon's character and actions throughout the Digimon series vividly illustrate Lilith's influence on embracing and integrating the shadow self. Her dark nature, powerful presence, and ability to challenge the DigiDestined make her a perfect embodiment of Lilith's qualities.

1. **Shadow Self**: LadyDevimon's dark and formidable nature represents the shadow self, encompassing repressed desires and fears. She embodies the parts of the psyche that are often hidden and feared, forcing the DigiDestined to confront these aspects. LadyDevimon's presence highlights the importance of acknowledging and embracing the shadow self, aligning with Lilith's themes of integration.

2. **Power and Independence**: LadyDevimon's autonomous and powerful presence reflects Lilith's emphasis on personal power and independence. She operates outside societal norms and restrictions, fully embracing her own strength and autonomy. LadyDevimon's rejection of conventional expectations mirrors Lilith's themes of empowerment and self-reliance.

3. **Taboo and Forbidden**: LadyDevimon's association with the dark and forbidden aspects of the self aligns with Lilith's connection to the taboo. Her seductive and mysterious nature challenges conventional morality, inviting the DigiDestined to explore the parts of themselves that are considered socially unacceptable. LadyDevimon's allure of the forbidden embodies Lilith's influence on confronting taboo desires.

4. **Confrontation and Integration**: LadyDevimon's role as an antagonist forces the DigiDestined to confront and integrate their shadow selves. Her presence compels them to face their inner fears and hidden desires, promoting personal growth and self-acceptance. LadyDevimon's ability to evoke confrontation and transformation highlights Lilith's themes of integration and growth through embracing the shadow self.

5. **Primal and Instinctual**: LadyDevimon's connection to primal and instinctual desires reflects Lilith's emphasis on raw emotions

and instincts. She embodies the untamed and instinctual aspects of the self, encouraging the DigiDestined to connect with their own primal nature. LadyDevimon's raw and powerful presence mirrors Lilith's influence on embracing our instinctual side.

6. **Mystery and Seduction**: LadyDevimon's mysterious and seductive allure embodies Lilith's qualities of mystery and seduction. Her enigmatic presence challenges the DigiDestined to explore the unknown and confront their own desires. LadyDevimon's seductive nature highlights Lilith's influence on embracing the allure of the forbidden and the mysteries of the self.

Conclusion

In "Digital Cosmos: The Astrological Digimon Compendium," LadyDevimon serves as a powerful representation of Lilith's qualities of embracing and integrating the shadow self. Her character, marked by darkness, power, and the ability to challenge and transform, mirrors Lilith's influence on our actions, values, and personal growth. Through LadyDevimon's role, we gain a deeper appreciation for the ways in which the digital and celestial realms intertwine, enriching our understanding of both Digimon and astrology.

As we continue to explore the Digital Cosmos, we recognize how various Digimon characters embody the traits and energies of different astrological signs and celestial events. Let LadyDevimon's embrace of the shadow self inspire us to confront our own hidden aspects, integrate our shadow, and transform our understanding of ourselves, revealing the profound connections between the worlds of Digimon and astrology.

Part 4: Moon Phases and Their Digital Influences

Chapter 27: New Moon: Beginnings with DemiVeemon
Characteristics of the New Moon in Astrology

The New Moon marks the beginning of the lunar cycle and symbolizes new beginnings, fresh starts, and the planting of seeds for future growth. In astrology, the New Moon is a powerful time for setting intentions, initiating projects, and embracing new opportunities. It represents a period of renewal and potential, where the energy is ripe for starting anew and embarking on new ventures.

Key characteristics of the New Moon in astrology include:

- **New Beginnings**: The New Moon signifies the start of a new cycle, making it an ideal time for new beginnings and fresh starts.
- **Initiation and Potential**: It represents the initiation of new projects, ideas, and ventures, highlighting the potential for growth and development.
- **Intention Setting**: The energy of the New Moon is perfect for setting intentions and goals for the upcoming cycle.
- **Renewal and Rebirth**: It embodies the themes of renewal and rebirth, offering a chance to shed the old and embrace the new.
- **Hope and Optimism**: The New Moon brings a sense of hope and optimism, encouraging us to look forward to the possibilities ahead.
- **Growth and Development**: It lays the groundwork for future growth and development, emphasizing the importance of nurturing new beginnings.

DemiVeemon's Role in New Beginnings and Potential

DemiVeemon, the playful and eager Digimon, represents new beginnings and untapped potential. As the In-Training form of Veemon, DemiVeemon embodies the qualities of innocence, curiosity, and the promise of growth. His role in the Digimon series highlights the excitement and potential that come with new beginnings, making him a symbol of the New Moon's energy.

Key attributes of DemiVeemon's role in new beginnings and potential include:

- **Innocence and Curiosity**: DemiVeemon's innocent and curious nature reflects the fresh start and exploration associated with new beginnings.
- **Playfulness and Joy**: His playful demeanor brings a sense of joy and lightheartedness, embodying the hope and optimism of the New Moon.
- **Potential for Growth**: As the In-Training form of Veemon, DemiVeemon holds significant potential for growth and development, symbolizing the initiation of new ventures.
- **Eagerness to Learn**: DemiVeemon's eagerness to learn and explore new experiences aligns with the New Moon's emphasis on setting intentions and embracing new opportunities.
- **Supportive and Loyal**: Despite his small size, DemiVeemon is supportive and loyal, providing a foundation for future strength and resilience.
- **Transformation and Evolution**: His eventual evolution into Veemon and more powerful forms highlights the themes of renewal, growth, and the unfolding of potential.

How DemiVeemon Reflects the New Moon's Energy of Initiation and Fresh Starts

DemiVeemon's character and actions throughout the Digimon series vividly illustrate the New Moon's influence on new beginnings, potential, and the initiation of fresh starts. His playful nature, curiosity, and promise of growth make him a perfect embodiment of the New Moon's qualities.

1. **New Beginnings**: DemiVeemon's role as an In-Training Digimon represents the start of a new cycle, embodying the essence of new beginnings. His presence signifies a fresh start and the excitement of embarking on new adventures. DemiVeemon's journey highlights the importance of embracing new opportunities, reflecting the New Moon's energy of renewal and initiation.

2. **Initiation and Potential**: DemiVeemon's potential for growth and development aligns with the New Moon's emphasis on initiating new projects and ventures. He symbolizes the beginning stages of Veemon's evolution, showcasing the promise and potential inherent in new beginnings. DemiVeemon's journey from In-Training to Champion forms highlights the importance of nurturing new starts to achieve future success.

3. **Intention Setting**: DemiVeemon's curious and eager nature reflects the New Moon's focus on setting intentions and goals. His desire to learn and grow aligns with the process of setting clear intentions during the New Moon phase. DemiVeemon's actions emphasize the importance of planning and preparing for future growth, embodying the New Moon's themes of intention setting and potential.

4. **Renewal and Rebirth**: DemiVeemon's evolution and transformation symbolize the themes of renewal and rebirth associated with the New Moon. Each stage of his growth represents a fresh start and the shedding of old limitations. DemiVeemon's ability to transform and evolve highlights the New Moon's influence on renewal and the continuous cycle of growth and development.

5. **Hope and Optimism**: DemiVeemon's playful and joyful demeanor brings a sense of hope and optimism, mirroring the New Moon's positive energy. His presence encourages those around him to look forward to new possibilities and embrace the excitement of fresh starts. DemiVeemon's cheerful nature embodies the optimism and hope that accompany new beginnings.

6. **Growth and Development**: DemiVeemon's journey from In-Training to more powerful forms underscores the importance of growth and development. His evolution represents the nurturing and cultivation of new beginnings to achieve greater potential. DemiVeemon's growth reflects the New Moon's energy of laying the groundwork for future success and development.

Conclusion

In "Digital Cosmos: The Astrological Digimon Compendium," DemiVeemon serves as a powerful representation of the New Moon's qualities of new beginnings, potential, and the initiation of fresh starts. His character, marked by innocence, curiosity, and the promise of growth, mirrors the New Moon's influence on our actions, values, and aspirations. Through DemiVeemon's journey, we gain a deeper appreciation for the ways in which the digital and celestial realms intertwine, enriching our understanding of both Digimon and astrology.

As we continue to explore the Digital Cosmos, we recognize how various Digimon characters embody the traits and energies of different astrological signs and celestial events. Let DemiVeemon's playful spirit and potential for growth inspire us to embrace new beginnings, set clear intentions, and nurture our dreams, revealing the profound connections between the worlds of Digimon and astrology.

Chapter 28: Waxing Crescent: Growth with Gabumon
Characteristics of the Waxing Crescent in Astrology

The Waxing Crescent Moon phase occurs after the New Moon and signifies the initial stages of growth and development. In astrology, this phase is associated with setting intentions into motion, taking actionable steps towards goals, and experiencing visible progress. The energy of the Waxing Crescent is one of expansion, momentum, and the nurturing of new ideas and projects as they begin to take shape.

Key characteristics of the Waxing Crescent in astrology include:

- **Growth and Expansion**: The Waxing Crescent symbolizes the early stages of growth, where initial efforts start to show results.
- **Momentum and Progress**: It represents building momentum and making steady progress towards goals and aspirations.
- **Nurturing Intentions**: This phase is about nurturing the seeds planted during the New Moon, ensuring they have the support needed to grow.
- **Optimism and Confidence**: The Waxing Crescent brings a sense of optimism and confidence, encouraging action and forward movement.
- **Building Foundations**: It emphasizes laying the groundwork and establishing strong foundations for future success.
- **Exploration and Learning**: This phase is a time for exploring new opportunities, learning, and adapting to ensure continued growth.

Gabumon's Role in Growth and Development

Gabumon, the wolf-like Digimon, plays a significant role in growth and development within the Digimon series. As the partner Digimon of Matt Ishida, Gabumon exhibits traits of loyalty, perseverance, and support, essential for the journey of growth. His evolution into Garurumon and later into MetalGarurumon showcases his potential for progress and the nurturing of his abilities, reflecting the qualities of the Waxing Crescent phase.

Key attributes of Gabumon's role in growth and development include:

- **Support and Loyalty**: Gabumon's unwavering support and loyalty to Matt and the other DigiDestined provide a strong foundation for their growth.
- **Perseverance and Determination**: He demonstrates perseverance and determination, essential for overcoming obstacles and achieving progress.
- **Evolving Abilities**: Gabumon's evolution into more powerful forms highlights his capacity for growth and development.
- **Encouragement and Motivation**: His presence and encouragement motivate the DigiDestined to pursue their goals and continue their journey.
- **Adaptability and Learning**: Gabumon's adaptability and willingness to learn new skills reflect the exploratory nature of the Waxing Crescent phase.
- **Foundation Building**: He helps lay the groundwork for the DigiDestined's success, ensuring they have the support and resources needed for their journey.

How Gabumon Channels the Waxing Crescent's Energy of Expansion and Progress

Gabumon's character and actions throughout the Digimon series vividly illustrate the Waxing Crescent's influence on growth, expansion, and progress. His supportive nature, determination, and evolving abilities make him a perfect embodiment of the Waxing Crescent's qualities.

1. **Growth and Expansion**: Gabumon's journey from his Rookie form to his powerful evolutions into Garurumon and MetalGarurumon represents the essence of growth and expansion. Each

stage of his evolution signifies a step forward in his development, reflecting the Waxing Crescent's energy of nurturing and expanding new beginnings. Gabumon's continuous growth highlights the importance of ongoing development and progress.

2. **Momentum and Progress**: Gabumon's perseverance and determination in battles and challenges align with the Waxing Crescent's focus on building momentum and making progress. His efforts contribute significantly to the DigiDestined's successes, pushing them forward in their journey. Gabumon's role in maintaining momentum and achieving progress embodies the Waxing Crescent's dynamic energy.

3. **Nurturing Intentions**: Gabumon's support and loyalty provide a nurturing environment for the DigiDestined, helping them to cultivate their goals and intentions. His unwavering support ensures that the seeds of their aspirations are nurtured and given the necessary care to grow. Gabumon's nurturing presence reflects the Waxing Crescent's emphasis on supporting and developing new ideas.

4. **Optimism and Confidence**: Gabumon's positive attitude and encouragement inspire confidence and optimism in the DigiDestined. His belief in their abilities and potential motivates them to take action and pursue their goals with confidence. Gabumon's ability to foster optimism and confidence highlights the Waxing Crescent's uplifting and motivating energy.

5. **Building Foundations**: Gabumon's role in laying the groundwork for the DigiDestined's success aligns with the Waxing Crescent's focus on building strong foundations. He helps establish the necessary support systems and resources, ensuring that the DigiDestined have a solid base from which to grow. Gabumon's foundational support embodies the Waxing Crescent's emphasis on creating a stable platform for future success.

6. **Exploration and Learning**: Gabumon's adaptability and willingness to learn new skills reflect the exploratory and learning-

oriented nature of the Waxing Crescent phase. He continuously seeks to improve and adapt, ensuring that he can meet the challenges of their journey. Gabumon's commitment to exploration and learning highlights the importance of growth through new experiences and knowledge.

Conclusion

In "Digital Cosmos: The Astrological Digimon Compendium," Gabumon serves as a powerful representation of the Waxing Crescent's qualities of growth, expansion, and progress. His character, marked by loyalty, perseverance, and evolving abilities, mirrors the Waxing Crescent's influence on our actions, values, and aspirations. Through Gabumon's journey, we gain a deeper appreciation for the ways in which the digital and celestial realms intertwine, enriching our understanding of both Digimon and astrology.

As we continue to explore the Digital Cosmos, we recognize how various Digimon characters embody the traits and energies of different astrological signs and celestial events. Let Gabumon's supportive presence and determination inspire us to embrace growth, nurture our intentions, and make steady progress towards our goals, revealing the profound connections between the worlds of Digimon and astrology.

Chapter 29: First Quarter: Challenges with Gatomon
Characteristics of the First Quarter in Astrology

The First Quarter Moon phase occurs halfway between the New Moon and the Full Moon. It is a time of action, decision-making, and overcoming challenges. In astrology, this phase is associated with facing obstacles that test our commitment to the goals and intentions set during the New Moon. The energy of the First Quarter is dynamic and assertive, encouraging us to make decisions, take decisive action, and address any issues that may impede our progress.

Key characteristics of the First Quarter in astrology include:

- **Action and Initiative**: The First Quarter Moon prompts us to take action and move forward with our plans.
- **Decision-Making**: It is a time for making important decisions that will influence the direction of our efforts.
- **Overcoming Obstacles**: This phase involves facing and overcoming challenges that stand in the way of our progress.
- **Building Momentum**: The First Quarter helps build momentum, pushing us to stay focused and driven.
- **Testing Commitment**: It tests our commitment to our goals, ensuring we are dedicated and willing to put in the effort required.
- **Adaptability and Problem-Solving**: This phase requires adaptability and problem-solving skills to navigate obstacles effectively.

Gatomon's Role in Overcoming Obstacles and Challenges

Gatomon, the feline Digimon, is known for her resilience, strength, and ability to overcome significant challenges. As the partner Digimon of Kari Kamiya, Gatomon exhibits traits of determination, adaptability, and strategic thinking. Her journey from a dark past under Myotismon's control to becoming a trusted and powerful ally highlights her role in facing and overcoming obstacles, reflecting the qualities of the First Quarter phase.

Key attributes of Gatomon's role in overcoming obstacles and challenges include:

- **Resilience and Strength**: Gatomon's resilience and strength enable her to face and overcome numerous challenges.
- **Adaptability and Resourcefulness**: She demonstrates adaptability and resourcefulness in difficult situations, finding ways to navigate obstacles.
- **Courage and Determination**: Gatomon's courage and determination drive her to confront and overcome adversities.
- **Strategic Thinking**: She uses strategic thinking to make important decisions and take decisive action.
- **Support and Protection**: Gatomon provides support and protection to Kari and the DigiDestined, helping them face their own challenges.
- **Transformation and Redemption**: Her journey of transformation and redemption showcases her ability to overcome past difficulties and grow stronger.

How Gatomon Embodies the First Quarter's Themes of Action and Decision-Making

Gatomon's character and actions throughout the Digimon series vividly illustrate the First Quarter's influence on action, decision-making, and overcoming challenges. Her resilience, strategic thinking, and adaptability make her a perfect embodiment of the First Quarter's qualities.

1. **Action and Initiative**: Gatomon's proactive nature and readiness to take action align with the First Quarter's emphasis on initiative. She is always prepared to step forward and confront challenges head-on, embodying the dynamic and assertive energy

of this lunar phase. Gatomon's decisive actions drive the DigiDestined's progress, ensuring they remain focused and motivated.

2. **Decision-Making**: Gatomon's ability to make important decisions in critical moments reflects the First Quarter's focus on decision-making. Her strategic thinking and quick judgment are crucial in navigating obstacles and ensuring the success of their missions. Gatomon's decision-making skills highlight the importance of making timely and effective choices to overcome challenges.

3. **Overcoming Obstacles**: Gatomon's journey is marked by numerous obstacles that test her strength and resilience. Her ability to confront and overcome these challenges embodies the First Quarter's theme of facing and surmounting difficulties. Gatomon's determination and perseverance demonstrate the power of resilience in achieving progress.

4. **Building Momentum**: Gatomon's actions help build momentum for the DigiDestined, driving their efforts forward and ensuring continuous progress. Her energy and determination inspire her teammates to stay focused and committed to their goals. Gatomon's role in maintaining momentum reflects the First Quarter's influence on sustaining drive and focus.

5. **Testing Commitment**: The challenges Gatomon faces test her commitment to her friends and their mission. Her unwavering dedication and willingness to overcome any obstacle illustrate the First Quarter's role in testing and strengthening our commitment to our goals. Gatomon's steadfast loyalty and perseverance highlight the importance of dedication and effort.

6. **Adaptability and Problem-Solving**: Gatomon's adaptability and problem-solving skills are essential in navigating the obstacles she encounters. She finds creative solutions and adapts to changing circumstances, embodying the First Quarter's emphasis on flexibility and resourcefulness. Gatomon's ability to adapt and

solve problems effectively showcases the importance of these qualities in overcoming challenges.

Conclusion

In "Digital Cosmos: The Astrological Digimon Compendium," Gatomon serves as a powerful representation of the First Quarter's qualities of action, decision-making, and overcoming challenges. Her character, marked by resilience, strategic thinking, and adaptability, mirrors the First Quarter's influence on our actions, values, and progress. Through Gatomon's journey, we gain a deeper appreciation for the ways in which the digital and celestial realms intertwine, enriching our understanding of both Digimon and astrology.

As we continue to explore the Digital Cosmos, we recognize how various Digimon characters embody the traits and energies of different astrological signs and celestial events. Let Gatomon's resilience and determination inspire us to take decisive action, make important decisions, and overcome the challenges we face, revealing the profound connections between the worlds of Digimon and astrology.

Chapter 30: Waxing Gibbous: Refinement with Angewomon
Characteristics of the Waxing Gibbous in Astrology

The Waxing Gibbous Moon phase occurs between the First Quarter and the Full Moon, representing a time of refinement, preparation, and fine-tuning. In astrology, this phase is associated with honing skills, perfecting plans, and making necessary adjustments to ensure success. The Waxing Gibbous energy is about building on the progress made so far and preparing for the culmination of efforts. It encourages us to review, revise, and improve our actions and strategies to achieve the best possible outcomes.

Key characteristics of the Waxing Gibbous in astrology include:

- **Refinement and Perfection**: The Waxing Gibbous phase is a time for refining and perfecting efforts, ensuring everything is in optimal condition.
- **Preparation and Readiness**: It emphasizes the importance of preparation and readiness for the upcoming culmination of goals.
- **Review and Adjustment**: This phase involves reviewing progress and making necessary adjustments to improve results.
- **Attention to Detail**: The Waxing Gibbous phase encourages paying attention to details and fine-tuning plans and actions.
- **Building Momentum**: It focuses on building momentum and ensuring that efforts are aligned and moving towards successful completion.
- **Patience and Persistence**: This phase requires patience and persistence, emphasizing the need to continue working diligently and methodically.

Angewomon's Role in Refining and Improving Situations

Angewomon, the angelic Digimon, is known for her role in refining and improving situations. As the ultimate form of Gatomon, Angewomon exhibits traits of grace, precision, and strategic enhancement. Her presence brings a sense of purity and perfection, often turning the tide in battles and leading the DigiDestined towards success. Angewomon's ability to refine and elevate situations aligns her with the qualities of the Waxing Gibbous phase.

Key attributes of Angewomon's role in refining and improving situations include:

- **Grace and Precision**: Angewomon's actions are marked by grace and precision, ensuring that her interventions are effective and impactful.
- **Strategic Enhancement**: She strategically enhances the capabilities of her allies, providing support and strength exactly where it is needed.
- **Healing and Purification**: Angewomon's healing abilities help restore and purify, improving the overall condition of her environment and companions.
- **Attention to Detail**: Her meticulous approach ensures that all aspects of a situation are considered and addressed, leading to refined outcomes.
- **Support and Guidance**: Angewomon provides support and guidance to the DigiDestined, helping them refine their strategies and actions.
- **Persistence and Patience**: She embodies persistence and patience, continuously working towards the improvement and perfection of efforts.

How Angewomon Reflects the Waxing Gibbous's Energy of Refinement and Preparation

Angewomon's character and actions throughout the Digimon series vividly illustrate the Waxing Gibbous's influence on refinement, preparation, and enhancement. Her grace, precision, and strategic support make her a perfect embodiment of the Waxing Gibbous's qualities.

1. **Refinement and Perfection**: Angewomon's interventions in battles and challenges often involve refining and perfecting the strategies of the DigiDestined. Her presence brings a sense of meticulousness and attention to detail, ensuring that actions are executed flawlessly. Angewomon's ability to refine and perfect outcomes embodies the Waxing Gibbous's emphasis on achieving optimal results.

2. **Preparation and Readiness**: Angewomon's role in preparing the DigiDestined for critical moments reflects the Waxing Gibbous's focus on preparation and readiness. She helps them anticipate challenges and equips them with the necessary tools and strategies to succeed. Angewomon's preparation and support highlight the importance of being ready for the culmination of efforts.

3. **Review and Adjustment**: Angewomon's strategic enhancements often involve reviewing and adjusting the DigiDestined's plans to ensure their effectiveness. She provides insightful guidance and makes necessary adjustments to improve their chances of success. Angewomon's role in reviewing and refining strategies aligns with the Waxing Gibbous's energy of fine-tuning and improvement.

4. **Attention to Detail**: Angewomon's meticulous approach to battles and challenges reflects the Waxing Gibbous's emphasis on attention to detail. She ensures that every aspect of a situation is considered and addressed, leading to refined and successful out-

comes. Angewomon's precision and care embody the importance of details in achieving perfection.

5. **Building Momentum**: Angewomon's actions help build momentum for the DigiDestined, driving their efforts forward and ensuring continuous progress. Her strategic support and enhancements keep the team focused and moving towards their goals. Angewomon's ability to maintain and build momentum reflects the Waxing Gibbous's influence on sustaining drive and progress.

6. **Patience and Persistence**: Angewomon's persistent and patient nature aligns with the Waxing Gibbous's qualities of patience and persistence. She continuously works towards improving and refining efforts, demonstrating the importance of persistence in achieving perfection. Angewomon's dedication and patience highlight the need for ongoing effort and refinement.

Conclusion

In "Digital Cosmos: The Astrological Digimon Compendium," Angewomon serves as a powerful representation of the Waxing Gibbous's qualities of refinement, preparation, and enhancement. Her character, marked by grace, precision, and strategic support, mirrors the Waxing Gibbous's influence on our actions, values, and aspirations. Through Angewomon's journey, we gain a deeper appreciation for the ways in which the digital and celestial realms intertwine, enriching our understanding of both Digimon and astrology.

As we continue to explore the Digital Cosmos, we recognize how various Digimon characters embody the traits and energies of different astrological signs and celestial events. Let Angewomon's graceful presence and meticulous refinement inspire us to hone our skills, perfect our strategies, and prepare diligently for success, revealing the profound connections between the worlds of Digimon and astrology.

Chapter 31: Full Moon: Fulfillment with WarGreymon
Characteristics of the Full Moon in Astrology

The Full Moon represents the peak of the lunar cycle and is a time of culmination, realization, and fulfillment. In astrology, the Full Moon is associated with bringing things to fruition, heightened emotions, and the illumination of truths. It signifies the completion of a cycle and the manifestation of intentions set during the New Moon. The energy of the Full Moon is intense and powerful, encouraging reflection on accomplishments and the celebration of successes.

Key characteristics of the Full Moon in astrology include:

- **Culmination and Completion**: The Full Moon marks the climax of the lunar cycle, symbolizing the completion and fulfillment of goals and intentions.
- **Realization and Manifestation**: It represents the manifestation of efforts and the realization of dreams and aspirations.
- **Illumination and Clarity**: The Full Moon brings heightened clarity and insight, illuminating truths and revealing hidden aspects.
- **Emotional Intensity**: It is a time of heightened emotions, often bringing feelings to the surface for acknowledgment and release.
- **Celebration and Reflection**: The Full Moon encourages celebration of achievements and reflection on the journey taken to reach fulfillment.
- **Balance and Integration**: It emphasizes the importance of balance and the integration of lessons learned throughout the lunar cycle.

WarGreymon's Role in Achieving Goals and Completion

WarGreymon, the mega form of Agumon, is a symbol of strength, determination, and the achievement of ultimate goals. As one of the most powerful Digimon in the series, WarGreymon embodies the qualities necessary for achieving completion and realizing one's potential. His role in the Digimon series involves pivotal battles and the culmination of significant arcs, highlighting his connection to the Full Moon's energy of fulfillment and realization.

Key attributes of WarGreymon's role in achieving goals and completion include:

- **Strength and Determination**: WarGreymon's immense strength and unwavering determination drive him to achieve his goals and protect his allies.
- **Leadership and Courage**: He demonstrates exceptional leadership and courage, guiding the DigiDestined through critical moments and leading them to victory.
- **Ultimate Form**: As the ultimate evolution of Agumon, War-Greymon represents the peak of potential and the culmination of growth and development.
- **Resolution and Fulfillment**: His presence often marks the resolution of major conflicts and the fulfillment of the DigiDestined's objectives.
- **Balance and Wisdom**: WarGreymon embodies a balance of power and wisdom, using his abilities with discernment and strategic insight.
- **Transformation and Realization**: His evolution into War-Greymon symbolizes the realization of potential and the transformative power of achieving one's ultimate form.

How WarGreymon Channels the Full Moon's Energy of Culmination and Realization

WarGreymon's character and actions throughout the Digimon series vividly illustrate the Full Moon's influence on culmination, realization, and fulfillment. His strength, leadership, and ability to achieve ultimate goals make him a perfect embodiment of the Full Moon's qualities.

1. **Culmination and Completion**: WarGreymon's battles often represent the culmination of the DigiDestined's efforts and the completion of significant arcs in the series. His presence marks the climax of their journey, symbolizing the fulfillment of their goals. WarGreymon's role in achieving completion embodies the Full Moon's energy of bringing things to fruition.

2. **Realization and Manifestation**: WarGreymon's evolution from Agumon to his ultimate form signifies the realization of potential and the manifestation of strength and power. His transformation highlights the process of becoming and achieving one's true form, reflecting the Full Moon's theme of realization and manifestation. WarGreymon's presence illustrates the fulfillment of intentions set at the beginning of the journey.

3. **Illumination and Clarity**: WarGreymon's role in pivotal battles often brings clarity and resolution to conflicts, illuminating truths and revealing hidden strengths. His decisive actions provide insight and understanding, aligning with the Full Moon's emphasis on illumination and clarity. WarGreymon's ability to bring light to dark situations mirrors the Full Moon's power to reveal and clarify.

4. **Emotional Intensity**: The intense battles and critical moments involving WarGreymon evoke heightened emotions, reflecting the Full Moon's influence on emotional intensity. His presence amplifies the emotional stakes, bringing feelings to the surface and prompting acknowledgment and release. WarGreymon's impact on the emotional landscape of the series embodies the Full Moon's intensity.

5. **Celebration and Reflection**: WarGreymon's victories often lead to moments of celebration and reflection for the DigiDestined. His successes mark significant achievements and provide opportunities to reflect on the journey taken to reach those points. WarGreymon's role in celebrating accomplishments and

reflecting on progress aligns with the Full Moon's themes of celebration and reflection.

6. **Balance and Integration**: WarGreymon's balance of power and wisdom highlights the importance of integrating lessons learned throughout the journey. His strategic use of abilities and thoughtful leadership demonstrate the integration of experience and knowledge. WarGreymon's ability to balance strength and wisdom reflects the Full Moon's emphasis on balance and integration.

Conclusion

In "Digital Cosmos: The Astrological Digimon Compendium," WarGreymon serves as a powerful representation of the Full Moon's qualities of culmination, realization, and fulfillment. His character, marked by strength, leadership, and the achievement of ultimate goals, mirrors the Full Moon's influence on our actions, values, and aspirations. Through WarGreymon's journey, we gain a deeper appreciation for the ways in which the digital and celestial realms intertwine, enriching our understanding of both Digimon and astrology.

As we continue to explore the Digital Cosmos, we recognize how various Digimon characters embody the traits and energies of different astrological signs and celestial events. Let WarGreymon's powerful presence and ultimate fulfillment inspire us to achieve our goals, celebrate our successes, and reflect on our journeys, revealing the profound connections between the worlds of Digimon and astrology.

Chapter 32: Waning Gibbous: Gratitude with Patamon
Characteristics of the Waning Gibbous in Astrology

The Waning Gibbous Moon phase occurs after the Full Moon and represents a time of reflection, gratitude, and dissemination of knowledge. In astrology, this phase is associated with the process of reviewing and integrating the experiences and insights gained during the Full Moon. It is a period of giving thanks, sharing wisdom, and teaching others. The energy of the Waning Gibbous encourages us to reflect on our achievements, express gratitude for what we have accomplished, and disseminate the knowledge we have gained.

Key characteristics of the Waning Gibbous in astrology include:

- **Reflection and Integration**: The Waning Gibbous phase is a time for reflecting on accomplishments and integrating the lessons learned.
- **Gratitude and Appreciation**: It emphasizes the importance of expressing gratitude and appreciating the journey and its outcomes.
- **Sharing Wisdom**: This phase encourages the sharing of knowledge and experiences with others, acting as a teacher and guide.
- **Review and Analysis**: The Waning Gibbous involves reviewing and analyzing what has been achieved, providing insights for future endeavors.
- **Generosity and Community**: It fosters a sense of generosity and community, encouraging the support and upliftment of others.

- **Preparation for Release**: This phase prepares us for the final stages of the lunar cycle, emphasizing the importance of letting go and preparing for renewal.

Patamon's Role in Expressing Gratitude and Sharing Wisdom

Patamon, the small, flying Digimon with big ears, plays a significant role in expressing gratitude, sharing wisdom, and acting as a guide. As the partner Digimon of T.K. Takaishi, Patamon exhibits traits of gentleness, wisdom, and an appreciative spirit. His journey from his Rookie form to his powerful evolution as Angemon and MagnaAngemon highlights his role in teaching valuable lessons and expressing gratitude for the support and love of his friends.

Key attributes of Patamon's role in expressing gratitude and sharing wisdom include:

- **Gentleness and Kindness**: Patamon's gentle and kind nature makes him a source of comfort and support for his friends.
- **Wisdom and Insight**: He often provides wisdom and insight, helping the DigiDestined navigate their challenges and learn important lessons.
- **Gratitude and Appreciation**: Patamon frequently expresses gratitude for the companionship and support of T.K. and the other DigiDestined.
- **Transformative Evolution**: His evolution into Angemon and MagnaAngemon signifies the profound impact of his growth and the wisdom he gains along the way.
- **Support and Guidance**: Patamon acts as a guide, offering support and guidance to his friends, especially during difficult times.
- **Teaching and Sharing**: He shares his knowledge and experiences, helping others understand the importance of gratitude and reflection.

How Patamon Embodies the Waning Gibbous's Themes of Reflection and Dissemination

Patamon's character and actions throughout the Digimon series vividly illustrate the Waning Gibbous's influence on reflection, gratitude, and the sharing of wisdom. His gentle nature, insightful guidance, and appreciative spirit make him a perfect embodiment of the Waning Gibbous's qualities.

1. **Reflection and Integration**: Patamon's journey involves reflecting on his experiences and integrating the lessons learned. His evolution into Angemon and MagnaAngemon represents the culmination of his growth and the integration of his wisdom. Patamon's reflective nature and his ability to learn from his experiences embody the Waning Gibbous's focus on reflection and integration.

2. **Gratitude and Appreciation**: Patamon frequently expresses gratitude for the support and friendship of T.K. and the other DigiDestined. His appreciative spirit and kind words highlight the importance of gratitude in fostering strong relationships and personal growth. Patamon's expressions of gratitude reflect the Waning Gibbous's emphasis on appreciating and giving thanks for achievements and support.

3. **Sharing Wisdom**: Patamon often shares his wisdom and insights with the DigiDestined, helping them navigate challenges and learn important lessons. His role as a teacher and guide aligns with the Waning Gibbous's theme of disseminating knowledge and experiences. Patamon's ability to impart wisdom and support others mirrors the importance of sharing and teaching during this lunar phase.

4. **Review and Analysis**: Patamon's reflective nature involves reviewing and analyzing his experiences, providing valuable insights for future endeavors. His thoughtful approach to challenges and his ability to draw lessons from his journey embody the Waning

Gibbous's focus on review and analysis. Patamon's analytical mind and his ability to offer thoughtful guidance highlight the importance of reflection.

5. **Generosity and Community**: Patamon's supportive and generous nature fosters a sense of community and mutual support among the DigiDestined. His willingness to help and uplift others aligns with the Waning Gibbous's emphasis on generosity and community. Patamon's actions illustrate the importance of supporting and sharing with others to build strong, cohesive bonds.

6. **Preparation for Release**: Patamon's journey also involves preparing for the final stages of the lunar cycle, emphasizing the importance of letting go and preparing for renewal. His role in helping the DigiDestined move forward and embrace new beginnings reflects the Waning Gibbous's focus on preparing for release and renewal. Patamon's guidance helps his friends transition smoothly through various stages of their journey.

Conclusion

In "Digital Cosmos: The Astrological Digimon Compendium," Patamon serves as a powerful representation of the Waning Gibbous's qualities of reflection, gratitude, and the sharing of wisdom. His character, marked by gentleness, insight, and an appreciative spirit, mirrors the Waning Gibbous's influence on our actions, values, and personal growth. Through Patamon's journey, we gain a deeper appreciation for the ways in which the digital and celestial realms intertwine, enriching our understanding of both Digimon and astrology.

As we continue to explore the Digital Cosmos, we recognize how various Digimon characters embody the traits and energies of different astrological signs and celestial events. Let Patamon's gentle presence and wise guidance inspire us to reflect on our achievements, express gratitude, and share our wisdom with others, revealing the profound connections between the worlds of Digimon and astrology.

Chapter 33: Last Quarter: Release with Beelzemon
Characteristics of the Last Quarter in Astrology

The Last Quarter Moon phase occurs between the Waning Gibbous and the New Moon, representing a time of release, transition, and transformation. In astrology, this phase is associated with letting go of what no longer serves us, reflecting on the past cycle, and preparing for new beginnings. The energy of the Last Quarter encourages us to evaluate our progress, release unnecessary burdens, and make space for future growth.

Key characteristics of the Last Quarter in astrology include:

- **Release and Letting Go**: The Last Quarter phase is a time for letting go of outdated beliefs, habits, and situations that hinder progress.
- **Reflection and Evaluation**: It emphasizes the importance of reflecting on the past cycle and evaluating what worked and what didn't.
- **Transition and Transformation**: This phase involves a period of transition and transformation, preparing for new beginnings.
- **Reassessment and Realignment**: The Last Quarter encourages reassessment and realignment of goals and intentions, ensuring they align with our true path.
- **Clearing and Purification**: It focuses on clearing away the old to make space for the new, promoting purification and renewal.
- **Acceptance and Forgiveness**: This phase fosters acceptance and forgiveness, helping to release emotional and mental burdens.

Beelzemon's Role in Letting Go and Transformation

Beelzemon, the formidable and complex Digimon, embodies the themes of release, letting go, and transformation. As the Mega form of Impmon, Beelzemon's journey is marked by significant challenges, redemption, and profound personal growth. His transformation from a dark, power-hungry Digimon to a redeemed ally highlights his role in letting go of past mistakes and embracing change.

Key attributes of Beelzemon's role in letting go and transformation include:

- **Redemption and Transformation**: Beelzemon's journey from Impmon to his powerful form symbolizes profound personal transformation and redemption.
- **Letting Go of the Past**: He must confront and release his past mistakes, guilt, and negative behaviors to move forward.
- **Inner Strength and Growth**: Beelzemon's inner strength and determination drive his growth and evolution, highlighting the power of transformation.
- **Acceptance and Forgiveness**: His journey involves accepting his past and seeking forgiveness, both from others and himself.
- **Guidance and Support**: Beelzemon ultimately becomes a guide and support for others, using his experiences to help them navigate their own challenges.
- **Reevaluation and Realignment**: His transformation requires reevaluating his goals and intentions, realigning them with a path of redemption and growth.

How Beelzemon Represents the Last Quarter's Energy of Release and Transition

Beelzemon's character and actions throughout the Digimon series vividly illustrate the Last Quarter's influence on release, transition, and transformation. His journey of redemption, letting go of the past, and embracing change make him a perfect embodiment of the Last Quarter's qualities.

1. **Release and Letting Go**: Beelzemon's journey involves letting go of his past mistakes, guilt, and negative behaviors. His trans-

formation from Impmon to Beelzemon requires releasing the desire for power and control, allowing him to embrace a path of redemption. Beelzemon's ability to let go and release the past embodies the Last Quarter's energy of clearing and purification.

2. **Reflection and Evaluation**: Beelzemon's journey is marked by deep reflection and evaluation of his actions and choices. He must confront the consequences of his past behaviors and assess the impact they have had on himself and others. Beelzemon's reflective nature highlights the Last Quarter's emphasis on evaluating the past cycle and learning from it.

3. **Transition and Transformation**: Beelzemon's transformation from a dark, power-hungry Digimon to a redeemed ally represents the Last Quarter's theme of transition and transformation. His journey involves profound personal growth and change, preparing him for new beginnings and a brighter path. Beelzemon's evolution embodies the transformative power of the Last Quarter.

4. **Reassessment and Realignment**: Beelzemon's transformation requires reassessing his goals and intentions, realigning them with a path of redemption and growth. He must redefine his purpose and direction, ensuring they align with his true self and values. Beelzemon's reevaluation and realignment reflect the Last Quarter's focus on adjusting and realigning goals.

5. **Clearing and Purification**: Beelzemon's journey involves clearing away the old, negative aspects of himself to make space for renewal and growth. His transformation purifies his character, allowing him to emerge as a stronger, wiser, and more compassionate being. Beelzemon's purification process highlights the Last Quarter's emphasis on clearing and making space for the new.

6. **Acceptance and Forgiveness**: Beelzemon's path to redemption involves accepting his past and seeking forgiveness from others and himself. His journey requires embracing his mistakes and learning to forgive himself, promoting healing and growth.

Beelzemon's ability to accept and forgive embodies the Last Quarter's themes of acceptance and forgiveness.

Conclusion

In "Digital Cosmos: The Astrological Digimon Compendium," Beelzemon serves as a powerful representation of the Last Quarter's qualities of release, transition, and transformation. His character, marked by redemption, letting go of the past, and profound personal growth, mirrors the Last Quarter's influence on our actions, values, and personal development. Through Beelzemon's journey, we gain a deeper appreciation for the ways in which the digital and celestial realms intertwine, enriching our understanding of both Digimon and astrology.

As we conclude our exploration of the Digital Cosmos, we recognize how various Digimon characters embody the traits and energies of different astrological signs and celestial events. Let Beelzemon's transformative journey inspire us to release the past, embrace change, and prepare for new beginnings, revealing the profound connections between the worlds of Digimon and astrology.

Chapter 34: Waning Crescent: Rest with Calumon
Characteristics of the Waning Crescent in Astrology

The Waning Crescent Moon phase occurs just before the New Moon and symbolizes a time of rest, closure, and introspection. In astrology, this phase is associated with winding down, letting go, and preparing for new beginnings. It is a period of reflection, healing, and rejuvenation, where we gather our strength and prepare for the upcoming cycle. The energy of the Waning Crescent encourages quiet contemplation, rest, and the gentle release of what is no longer needed.

Key characteristics of the Waning Crescent in astrology include:

- **Rest and Rejuvenation**: The Waning Crescent phase is a time for rest, recuperation, and gathering energy for the next cycle.
- **Closure and Completion**: It represents the final stages of the lunar cycle, encouraging the completion of unfinished business and letting go.
- **Introspection and Reflection**: This phase involves deep introspection and reflection, providing insights and understanding from the past cycle.
- **Healing and Release**: The Waning Crescent promotes healing and the gentle release of emotional, mental, and physical burdens.
- **Preparation for New Beginnings**: It emphasizes the importance of preparing for the new cycle, creating space for new opportunities and growth.
- **Quiet Contemplation**: This phase encourages a quieter, more contemplative approach, focusing on inner peace and tranquility.

Calumon's Role in Rest and Rejuvenation

Calumon, the small, enigmatic Digimon, plays a significant role in promoting rest, rejuvenation, and the gentle release of burdens. As a key figure in Digimon Tamers, Calumon exhibits traits of innocence, tranquility, and a calming presence. His unique ability to induce Digivolution in other Digimon highlights his role in facilitating transformation and renewal, while his demeanor encourages peace and relaxation.

Key attributes of Calumon's role in rest and rejuvenation include:

- **Innocence and Tranquility**: Calumon's innocent and tranquil nature provides a calming influence on those around him.
- **Calming Presence**: His presence brings a sense of peace and relaxation, helping others to rest and rejuvenate.
- **Facilitating Transformation**: Calumon's ability to induce Digivolution symbolizes the potential for renewal and growth.
- **Encouraging Rest**: He often promotes rest and relaxation, encouraging others to take a break and gather their strength.
- **Healing Influence**: Calumon's gentle nature and calming energy contribute to emotional and mental healing.
- **Preparation for Renewal**: His influence helps prepare others for new beginnings, creating a sense of readiness for the upcoming cycle.

How Calumon Channels the Waning Crescent's Energy of Closure and Rest

Calumon's character and actions throughout the Digimon series vividly illustrate the Waning Crescent's influence on rest, closure, and preparation for new beginnings. His calming presence, gentle nature, and ability to facilitate transformation make him a perfect embodiment of the Waning Crescent's qualities.

1. **Rest and Rejuvenation**: Calumon's presence encourages rest and rejuvenation, providing a calming influence that helps others relax and recuperate. His gentle nature and tranquil demeanor create an environment conducive to rest, embodying the Waning Crescent's focus on gathering energy for the next cycle. Calumon's ability to promote rest and relaxation highlights the importance of taking time to rejuvenate.

2. **Closure and Completion**: Calumon's role in facilitating Digivolution and transformation represents the completion of cycles and the preparation for new beginnings. His influence helps other Digimon reach their full potential, symbolizing the closure of one phase and the readiness for the next. Calumon's ability to bring about transformation reflects the Waning Crescent's emphasis on closure and completion.

3. **Introspection and Reflection**: Calumon's presence often prompts introspection and reflection, encouraging others to look inward and gain insights from their experiences. His calming influence allows for quiet contemplation, providing the space needed for deep reflection and understanding. Calumon's role in promoting introspection aligns with the Waning Crescent's focus on reflection and gaining insights.

4. **Healing and Release**: Calumon's gentle nature and calming energy contribute to emotional and mental healing, helping others release their burdens. His influence promotes a sense of peace and tranquility, facilitating the gentle release of what is no longer needed. Calumon's healing presence embodies the Waning Crescent's emphasis on healing and letting go.

5. **Preparation for New Beginnings**: Calumon's ability to induce Digivolution and promote transformation helps prepare others for new beginnings. His influence creates a sense of readiness and anticipation for the upcoming cycle, ensuring that others are prepared for growth and renewal. Calumon's role in preparing for new opportunities aligns with the Waning Crescent's focus on creating space for new beginnings.

6. **Quiet Contemplation**: Calumon's tranquil presence encourages quiet contemplation, fostering an environment of inner peace and calm. His gentle demeanor and soothing influence allow for a more contemplative approach, focusing on inner tranquility and reflection. Calumon's ability to promote quiet

contemplation reflects the Waning Crescent's emphasis on peace and tranquility.

Conclusion

In "Digital Cosmos: The Astrological Digimon Compendium," Calumon serves as a powerful representation of the Waning Crescent's qualities of rest, closure, and preparation for new beginnings. His character, marked by innocence, tranquility, and a calming presence, mirrors the Waning Crescent's influence on our actions, values, and personal growth. Through Calumon's journey, we gain a deeper appreciation for the ways in which the digital and celestial realms intertwine, enriching our understanding of both Digimon and astrology.

As we conclude our exploration of the Digital Cosmos, we recognize how various Digimon characters embody the traits and energies of different astrological signs and celestial events. Let Calumon's calming presence and gentle influence inspire us to rest, reflect, and prepare for new beginnings, revealing the profound connections between the worlds of Digimon and astrology.

Part 5: Celestial Events and Digital Convergences

Chapter 35: Solar Eclipses: Transformation with BlackWar-Greymon

Characteristics of Solar Eclipses in Astrology

Solar Eclipses are powerful celestial events that occur when the Moon passes between the Earth and the Sun, temporarily blocking the Sun's light. In astrology, Solar Eclipses signify significant transformations, new beginnings, and profound changes. They mark pivotal moments in our lives, often bringing about sudden shifts and revealing hidden truths. The energy of a Solar Eclipse is intense and catalytic, pushing us to break free from the old and embrace new directions with clarity and purpose.

Key characteristics of Solar Eclipses in astrology include:

- **Transformation and Renewal**: Solar Eclipses symbolize dramatic transformation and the opportunity for renewal and rebirth.
- **Revelation and Clarity**: They bring hidden truths to light, providing clarity and insight into aspects of our lives that were previously obscured.
- **Sudden Changes**: The energy of Solar Eclipses often brings sudden and unexpected changes, propelling us into new paths.
- **Endings and Beginnings**: They mark the end of one cycle and the beginning of another, encouraging us to let go of the past and embrace new opportunities.
- **Catalysts for Growth**: Solar Eclipses act as catalysts for personal growth and evolution, challenging us to step out of our comfort zones.
- **Empowerment and Awakening**: They empower us to make significant changes and awaken to new possibilities and potentials.

BlackWarGreymon's Transformative Nature

BlackWarGreymon, the dark and powerful counterpart to WarGreymon, embodies the themes of transformation, revelation, and profound change. Created from the fusion of 100 Control Spires, BlackWarGreymon's existence is marked by a search for purpose, identity, and understanding. His journey involves confronting his own darkness and seeking redemption, highlighting the transformative power of facing and integrating one's shadow.

Key attributes of BlackWarGreymon's transformative nature include:

- **Powerful and Intense**: BlackWarGreymon's immense power and intensity reflect the catalytic energy of Solar Eclipses.
- **Search for Purpose**: His quest for purpose and identity mirrors the transformative journey of self-discovery and renewal.
- **Confronting Darkness**: BlackWarGreymon's struggle with his own darkness symbolizes the process of facing and integrating hidden aspects of the self.
- **Redemption and Growth**: His journey towards redemption and understanding showcases the potential for profound personal growth and change.
- **Sudden Shifts**: BlackWarGreymon's creation and existence bring sudden and dramatic changes to the Digital World, aligning with the unexpected nature of Solar Eclipses.
- **Empowerment through Transformation**: His evolution and quest for meaning highlight the empowerment that comes from embracing transformation and new beginnings.

How BlackWarGreymon Embodies the Powerful Changes Brought by Solar Eclipses

BlackWarGreymon's character and actions throughout the Digimon series vividly illustrate the transformative power and catalytic energy of Solar Eclipses. His intense journey of self-discovery, confrontation with darkness, and quest for redemption make him a perfect embodiment of the profound changes brought by Solar Eclipses.

1. **Transformation and Renewal**: BlackWarGreymon's existence is a testament to the power of transformation and renewal. Created from the fusion of 100 Control Spires, his journey is marked by a search for identity and purpose, reflecting the transformative energy of Solar Eclipses. BlackWarGreymon's ability to undergo profound change embodies the essence of renewal and rebirth.

2. **Revelation and Clarity**: BlackWarGreymon's quest for understanding and truth aligns with the revelatory nature of Solar Eclipses. His journey brings hidden truths to light, providing clarity and insight into his own existence and purpose. BlackWarGreymon's pursuit of truth highlights the importance of revelation and clarity in the process of transformation.

3. **Sudden Changes**: BlackWarGreymon's creation and actions bring sudden and unexpected changes to the Digital World. His presence disrupts the status quo, propelling the DigiDestined and other Digimon into new paths and challenges. BlackWarGreymon's impact on the Digital World mirrors the sudden and catalytic changes brought by Solar Eclipses.

4. **Endings and Beginnings**: BlackWarGreymon's journey marks the end of one cycle and the beginning of another, reflecting the dual nature of Solar Eclipses. His quest for redemption and purpose signifies the letting go of his dark past and the embrace of new possibilities. BlackWarGreymon's transformation highlights the importance of endings and beginnings in personal growth.

5. **Catalysts for Growth**: BlackWarGreymon's existence acts as a catalyst for growth and evolution for both himself and those around him. His challenges and confrontations push others to grow, adapt, and evolve. BlackWarGreymon's role as a catalyst aligns with the transformative power of Solar Eclipses in driving personal and collective growth.

6. **Empowerment and Awakening**: BlackWarGreymon's journey towards understanding and redemption empowers him to embrace his true potential and purpose. His evolution and quest for meaning awaken new possibilities and potentials within him. BlackWarGreymon's empowerment through transformation embodies the awakening energy of Solar Eclipses.

Conclusion

In "Digital Cosmos: The Astrological Digimon Compendium," BlackWarGreymon serves as a powerful representation of the transformative and catalytic energy of Solar Eclipses. His character, marked by intense power, a quest for purpose, and profound personal growth, mirrors the influence of Solar Eclipses on our actions, values, and personal evolution. Through BlackWarGreymon's journey, we gain a deeper appreciation for the ways in which the digital and celestial realms intertwine, enriching our understanding of both Digimon and astrology.

As we continue to explore the Digital Cosmos, we recognize how various Digimon characters embody the traits and energies of different astrological signs and celestial events. Let BlackWarGreymon's transformative journey inspire us to embrace the powerful changes brought by Solar Eclipses, confront our own shadows, and awaken to new possibilities and potentials, revealing the profound connections between the worlds of Digimon and astrology.

Chapter 36: Lunar Eclipses: Revelations with Magnadramon Characteristics of Lunar Eclipses in Astrology

Lunar Eclipses occur when the Earth passes between the Sun and the Moon, casting a shadow over the Moon. In astrology, Lunar Eclipses are associated with revelations, emotional intensity, and the culmination of cycles. They bring hidden truths to light and encourage us to confront our innermost feelings and unresolved issues. The energy of a Lunar Eclipse is profound and transformative, urging us to let go of what no longer serves us and embrace deeper understanding and clarity.

Key characteristics of Lunar Eclipses in astrology include:

- **Revelation and Illumination**: Lunar Eclipses illuminate hidden truths, providing clarity and insight into aspects of our lives that were previously obscured.
- **Emotional Intensity**: They heighten emotions and bring unresolved feelings to the surface for acknowledgment and release.
- **Culmination and Completion**: Lunar Eclipses mark the culmination of cycles, encouraging us to complete unfinished business and move forward.
- **Confrontation and Release**: They prompt us to confront deep-seated issues and release emotional, mental, and spiritual burdens.
- **Transformation and Change**: The energy of Lunar Eclipses is transformative, pushing us towards personal growth and evolution.
- **Insight and Understanding**: They enhance our ability to gain deep insights and understanding, promoting self-awareness and enlightenment.

Magnadramon's Role in Revealing Hidden Truths

Magnadramon, the majestic and powerful dragon Digimon, embodies the themes of revelation, illumination, and profound transformation. As the Mega form of Gatomon, Magnadramon is a symbol of ultimate strength, wisdom, and the power to unveil hidden truths. Her role in the Digimon series involves bringing clarity and understanding to critical situations, revealing the deeper truths that guide the DigiDestined towards their ultimate goals.

Key attributes of Magnadramon's role in revealing hidden truths include:

- **Majestic Presence**: Magnadramon's majestic and awe-inspiring presence commands attention and respect, symbolizing the power of revelation.
- **Wisdom and Insight**: Her deep wisdom and insight enable her to uncover hidden truths and provide clarity to the DigiDestined.
- **Transformative Power**: Magnadramon's evolution represents profound transformation and the culmination of Gatomon's growth and potential.
- **Emotional Depth**: Her connection to emotional and spiritual realms allows her to bring unresolved feelings to the surface for healing and release.
- **Guidance and Enlightenment**: Magnadramon provides guidance and enlightenment, helping the DigiDestined navigate their journeys with greater understanding.
- **Illumination of Truths**: Her actions and presence illuminate hidden aspects of challenges and conflicts, revealing the underlying truths.

How Magnadramon Channels the Revelatory Energy of Lunar Eclipses

Magnadramon's character and actions throughout the Digimon series vividly illustrate the revelatory and transformative power of Lunar Eclipses. Her majestic presence, profound wisdom, and ability to reveal hidden truths make her a perfect embodiment of the Lunar Eclipse's qualities.

1. **Revelation and Illumination**: Magnadramon's ability to unveil hidden truths and provide clarity aligns with the revelatory energy of Lunar Eclipses. Her deep wisdom and insight allow her to illuminate the underlying aspects of conflicts and challenges, guiding the DigiDestined towards greater understanding. Magnadramon's role in revealing truths embodies the illumination and clarity brought by Lunar Eclipses.

2. **Emotional Intensity**: Magnadramon's connection to emotional and spiritual realms heightens the emotional intensity of critical moments. Her presence brings unresolved feelings to the surface, encouraging acknowledgment and release. Magnadramon's ability to evoke and address deep emotions reflects the emotional intensity of Lunar Eclipses.

3. **Culmination and Completion**: Magnadramon's evolution represents the culmination of Gatomon's growth and the completion of her transformative journey. Her presence marks the culmination of critical arcs and the resolution of significant conflicts. Magnadramon's role in achieving completion and resolution aligns with the culmination and completion themes of Lunar Eclipses.

4. **Confrontation and Release**: Magnadramon's guidance often prompts the DigiDestined to confront deep-seated issues and release emotional and mental burdens. Her transformative power encourages them to let go of what no longer serves them and embrace change. Magnadramon's ability to facilitate confrontation and release embodies the transformative and purging energy of Lunar Eclipses.

5. **Transformation and Change**: Magnadramon's evolution and role in guiding the DigiDestined through transformative experiences highlight the profound change associated with Lunar

Eclipses. Her journey from Gatomon to Magnadramon symbolizes personal growth and evolution, reflecting the transformative power of Lunar Eclipses. Magnadramon's presence inspires profound personal change and renewal.

6. **Insight and Understanding**: Magnadramon's deep wisdom and insight enhance the DigiDestined's ability to gain profound understanding and self-awareness. Her guidance illuminates the path forward, promoting enlightenment and greater self-awareness. Magnadramon's ability to provide clarity and understanding mirrors the insightful energy of Lunar Eclipses.

Conclusion

In "Digital Cosmos: The Astrological Digimon Compendium," Magnadramon serves as a powerful representation of the revelatory and transformative energy of Lunar Eclipses. Her character, marked by majestic presence, profound wisdom, and the ability to reveal hidden truths, mirrors the influence of Lunar Eclipses on our actions, values, and personal growth. Through Magnadramon's journey, we gain a deeper appreciation for the ways in which the digital and celestial realms intertwine, enriching our understanding of both Digimon and astrology.

As we conclude our exploration of the Digital Cosmos, we recognize how various Digimon characters embody the traits and energies of different astrological signs and celestial events. Let Magnadramon's majestic presence and profound revelations inspire us to embrace the transformative power of Lunar Eclipses, confront our hidden truths, and achieve greater self-awareness and understanding, revealing the profound connections between the worlds of Digimon and astrology.

Chapter 37: Meteor Showers: Inspiration with Pegasusmon
Characteristics of Meteor Showers in Astrology

Meteor showers are celestial events where numerous meteors, or "shooting stars," are seen radiating from a single point in the night sky. In astrology, meteor showers are associated with bursts of inspiration, fleeting moments of clarity, and the arrival of sudden insights. These events are seen as harbingers of hope, wonder, and a reminder of the beauty and vastness of the cosmos. Meteor showers symbolize the transient nature of inspiration and the importance of seizing the moment when clarity and creativity strike.

Key characteristics of meteor showers in astrology include:

- **Inspiration and Creativity**: Meteor showers signify sudden bursts of inspiration and creativity, sparking new ideas and perspectives.
- **Hope and Wonder**: They evoke a sense of hope and wonder, reminding us of the beauty and mystery of the universe.
- **Clarity and Insight**: Meteor showers bring fleeting moments of clarity and insight, illuminating our path and providing guidance.
- **Transient Nature**: These events highlight the transient and ephemeral nature of inspiration, encouraging us to act quickly on our insights.
- **Renewal and Rejuvenation**: Meteor showers symbolize renewal and rejuvenation, inspiring us to refresh our perspectives and approaches.
- **Cosmic Connection**: They remind us of our connection to the cosmos and the continuous flow of energy and inspiration from the universe.

Pegasusmon's Role in Inspiring Hope and Wonder

Pegasusmon, the majestic and noble Digimon, embodies the themes of inspiration, hope, and wonder. As the Armor Digivolved form of Patamon, Pegasusmon represents a significant transformation and carries an aura of divine grace and strength. His presence in the Digimon series brings hope and courage to the DigiDestined, inspiring them to believe in themselves and their mission. Pegasusmon's ability to soar through the skies and his connection to celestial energy make him a perfect symbol of the inspirational and fleeting nature of meteor showers.

Key attributes of Pegasusmon's role in inspiring hope and wonder include:

- **Majestic Presence**: Pegasusmon's majestic and awe-inspiring presence evokes a sense of wonder and admiration.
- **Divine Grace and Strength**: His grace and strength inspire hope and courage, encouraging others to strive for their goals.
- **Connection to the Skies**: Pegasusmon's ability to fly and his connection to celestial energy symbolize the ethereal and inspirational qualities of meteor showers.
- **Inspiration and Motivation**: His presence and actions inspire the DigiDestined to believe in themselves and their mission.
- **Guidance and Clarity**: Pegasusmon provides guidance and clarity in critical moments, helping to illuminate the path forward.
- **Renewal and Transformation**: His transformation into Pegasusmon represents renewal and the embrace of new perspectives and strengths.

How Pegasusmon Reflects the Inspirational and Fleeting Nature of Meteor Showers

Pegasusmon's character and actions throughout the Digimon series vividly illustrate the inspirational and fleeting qualities of meteor showers. His majestic presence, ability to inspire hope, and connection to celestial energy make him a perfect embodiment of the themes associated with meteor showers.

1. **Inspiration and Creativity**: Pegasusmon's presence brings sudden bursts of inspiration and creativity to the DigiDestined. His arrival often marks pivotal moments where new ideas and strategies are needed. Pegasusmon's ability to spark creativity and inspire action reflects the sudden and inspirational nature of meteor showers.

2. **Hope and Wonder**: Pegasusmon's majestic and noble appearance evokes a sense of hope and wonder among the DigiDestined. His grace and strength provide encouragement and uplift spirits, reminding them of the beauty and possibilities within their journey. Pegasusmon's ability to inspire hope aligns with the awe and wonder brought by meteor showers.

3. **Clarity and Insight**: Pegasusmon provides moments of clarity and insight, illuminating the path forward for the DigiDestined. His guidance helps them navigate challenges and make informed decisions. Pegasusmon's role in providing clarity mirrors the fleeting moments of illumination and insight associated with meteor showers.

4. **Transient Nature**: The moments of inspiration and clarity provided by Pegasusmon are often fleeting, encouraging the DigiDestined to act quickly on their insights. His presence serves as a reminder to seize the moment and embrace opportunities as they arise. Pegasusmon's transient influence reflects the ephemeral nature of inspiration brought by meteor showers.

5. **Renewal and Rejuvenation**: Pegasusmon's transformation from Patamon symbolizes renewal and rejuvenation, inspiring the DigiDestined to refresh their perspectives and approaches. His ability to bring new energy and strength highlights the renewing qualities of meteor showers. Pegasusmon's transformation encourages embracing change and new beginnings.

6. **Cosmic Connection**: Pegasusmon's connection to the skies and celestial energy reinforces the sense of cosmic connection and continuity. His presence reminds the DigiDestined of their link

to the greater universe and the flow of inspiration from the cosmos. Pegasusmon's celestial qualities embody the cosmic connection emphasized by meteor showers.

Conclusion

In "Digital Cosmos: The Astrological Digimon Compendium," Pegasusmon serves as a powerful representation of the inspirational and fleeting qualities of meteor showers. His character, marked by majestic presence, divine grace, and the ability to inspire hope and wonder, mirrors the influence of meteor showers on our actions, values, and personal growth. Through Pegasusmon's journey, we gain a deeper appreciation for the ways in which the digital and celestial realms intertwine, enriching our understanding of both Digimon and astrology.

As we continue to explore the Digital Cosmos, we recognize how various Digimon characters embody the traits and energies of different astrological signs and celestial events. Let Pegasusmon's inspiring presence and fleeting moments of clarity encourage us to embrace the bursts of inspiration and creativity that come our way, seizing the moment and acting on our insights, revealing the profound connections between the worlds of Digimon and astrology.

Chapter 38: Comets: Change with Alphamon
Characteristics of Comets in Astrology

Comets are celestial objects composed of ice, dust, and rocky material that, when passing close to the Sun, display a visible atmosphere or coma and sometimes a tail. In astrology, comets are seen as harbingers of significant change, transformation, and new directions. They symbolize sudden, often dramatic shifts in energy and circumstances, acting as catalysts that shake up the status quo and herald new beginnings. Comets bring a powerful message of transformation, urging us to embrace change and step into new phases of our lives with courage and openness.

Key characteristics of comets in astrology include:

- **Harbingers of Change**: Comets signify the arrival of significant changes and the onset of new phases in life.
- **Catalysts for Transformation**: They act as catalysts that trigger profound transformations and shifts in perspective.
- **Sudden and Dramatic**: The energy of comets is often sudden and dramatic, bringing unexpected events that alter the course of our lives.
- **Revelation and Enlightenment**: Comets illuminate new paths and possibilities, providing revelations and insights that lead to growth.
- **Disruption and Renewal**: They disrupt old patterns and systems, making way for renewal and fresh starts.
- **Cosmic Messengers**: Comets are seen as messengers from the cosmos, bringing important messages and guiding us toward our true path.

Alphamon's Significance in Heralding Change

Alphamon, a powerful and enigmatic Royal Knight Digimon, embodies the transformative and catalytic energy associated with comets. As a leader among the Royal Knights, Alphamon's presence signals significant shifts and pivotal moments in the Digital World. His role involves guiding and protecting the Digital World while initiating and overseeing profound transformations. Alphamon's actions often herald the beginning of new eras and the dismantling of outdated systems, making him a powerful symbol of change and transformation.

Key attributes of Alphamon's significance in heralding change include:

- **Leadership and Authority**: Alphamon's position as a leader among the Royal Knights grants him authority to initiate significant changes.
- **Catalyst for Transformation**: His presence and actions often trigger profound transformations in the Digital World, leading to new beginnings.
- **Guidance and Protection**: Alphamon provides guidance and protection during times of change, ensuring the Digital World transitions smoothly.
- **Illumination of New Paths**: He reveals new paths and possibilities, guiding Digimon toward growth and enlightenment.
- **Disruption of the Status Quo**: Alphamon's actions disrupt outdated systems and patterns, paving the way for renewal and progress.
- **Embodiment of Cosmic Wisdom**: His connection to the cosmic forces and deep wisdom makes him a messenger of important revelations and insights.

How Alphamon Embodies the Transformative Influence of Comets

Alphamon's character and actions throughout the Digimon series vividly illustrate the transformative and catalytic influence of comets. His leadership, ability to initiate profound changes, and role as a guiding force make him a perfect embodiment of the themes associated with comets in astrology.

1. **Harbingers of Change**: Alphamon's arrival in the Digital World often signifies the onset of significant changes and new phases. His presence marks pivotal moments that alter the course of events, embodying the comet's role as a harbinger of change. Alphamon's ability to signal and initiate change reflects the transformative power of comets.

2. **Catalysts for Transformation**: Alphamon acts as a catalyst for profound transformations within the Digital World. His actions trigger shifts in perspective, leading to the dismantling of outdated systems and the emergence of new structures. Alphamon's transformative influence mirrors the catalytic energy of comets, which prompt significant and lasting changes.

3. **Sudden and Dramatic**: The impact of Alphamon's interventions is often sudden and dramatic, bringing unexpected events that challenge the status quo. His decisive actions and powerful presence create immediate and significant changes. Alphamon's ability to bring about sudden transformations reflects the dramatic nature of comets.

4. **Revelation and Enlightenment**: Alphamon provides revelations and insights that illuminate new paths and possibilities for the Digimon. His wisdom and guidance lead to greater understanding and enlightenment, helping others navigate through periods of change. Alphamon's role in providing clarity and insight aligns with the revelatory energy of comets.

5. **Disruption and Renewal**: Alphamon's actions disrupt old patterns and systems, making way for renewal and fresh starts. He challenges existing structures and promotes the development of new, more effective ways of being. Alphamon's ability to foster renewal and progress embodies the disruptive and renewing qualities of comets.

6. **Cosmic Messengers**: Alphamon's deep connection to cosmic forces and his role as a messenger of important revelations highlight his embodiment of comet energy. He brings messages of

transformation and guides the Digital World toward its true path. Alphamon's wisdom and cosmic insight reflect the role of comets as messengers from the universe.

Conclusion

In "Digital Cosmos: The Astrological Digimon Compendium," Alphamon serves as a powerful representation of the transformative and catalytic energy of comets. His character, marked by leadership, profound wisdom, and the ability to initiate significant changes, mirrors the influence of comets on our actions, values, and personal growth. Through Alphamon's journey, we gain a deeper appreciation for the ways in which the digital and celestial realms intertwine, enriching our understanding of both Digimon and astrology.

As we continue to explore the Digital Cosmos, we recognize how various Digimon characters embody the traits and energies of different astrological signs and celestial events. Let Alphamon's transformative presence and cosmic wisdom inspire us to embrace the powerful changes brought by comets, navigate sudden shifts with courage, and step into new phases of growth and enlightenment, revealing the profound connections between the worlds of Digimon and astrology.

Chapter 39: Planetary Alignments: Synergy with Omnimon Characteristics of Planetary Alignments in Astrology

Planetary alignments occur when two or more planets in the solar system align closely in a specific configuration. In astrology, these alignments are significant events that symbolize heightened synergy, unity, and powerful collective energy. They represent moments when different forces come together harmoniously, amplifying their strengths and creating opportunities for profound growth, transformation, and unity. Planetary alignments are seen as times of powerful integration, cooperation, and the realization of greater potentials through combined efforts.

Key characteristics of planetary alignments in astrology include:

- **Synergy and Unity**: Planetary alignments symbolize the coming together of different energies in a harmonious and synergistic way.
- **Amplification of Strengths**: They amplify the strengths and potentials of the individual planets involved, creating powerful collective energy.
- **Cooperation and Integration**: These events emphasize cooperation, integration, and the unification of diverse elements to achieve greater goals.
- **Transformation and Growth**: Planetary alignments often mark periods of significant transformation and growth, driven by the combined energies.
- **Opportunities and Realization**: They open up new opportunities and pathways for realizing potential and achieving collective aims.
- **Harmony and Balance**: Planetary alignments foster harmony and balance, encouraging the resolution of conflicts and the creation of cohesive, unified efforts.

Omnimon's Role in Unity and Synergy

Omnimon, a fusion of WarGreymon and MetalGarurumon, is a powerful symbol of unity and synergy within the Digimon universe. As a DNA Digivolution, Omnimon represents the ultimate integration of strength, abilities, and virtues from two distinct Digimon. His presence signifies the harmonious combination of different forces, leading to enhanced power and effectiveness. Omnimon's role involves leading and protecting the DigiDestined, uniting their efforts and guiding them towards victory.

Key attributes of Omnimon's role in unity and synergy include:

- **Fusion of Strengths**: Omnimon's creation from WarGreymon and MetalGarurumon symbolizes the fusion of their strengths and abilities into a single, powerful entity.
- **Unity and Cooperation**: His existence highlights the importance of unity and cooperation, demonstrating how combined efforts can achieve greater outcomes.
- **Leadership and Protection**: Omnimon serves as a leader and protector, guiding the DigiDestined through critical battles and ensuring their success.
- **Harmony and Balance**: His balanced combination of attributes from both Digimon reflects harmony and the effective integration of diverse elements.
- **Transformation and Empowerment**: Omnimon's transformation from two separate entities into a unified whole represents profound transformation and empowerment.
- **Symbol of Hope**: His presence inspires hope and confidence, showing that unity and synergy can overcome even the most formidable challenges.

How Omnimon Represents the Powerful and Harmonious Effects of Planetary Alignments

Omnimon's character and actions throughout the Digimon series vividly illustrate the powerful and harmonious effects of planetary alignments. His unity, synergy, and ability to amplify strengths through cooperation make him a perfect embodiment of the themes associated with planetary alignments in astrology.

1. **Synergy and Unity**: Omnimon's creation through the fusion of WarGreymon and MetalGarurumon exemplifies the synergy and unity that planetary alignments represent. His existence as a unified entity demonstrates the power of combining diverse strengths and abilities to create something greater. Omnimon's ability to integrate different forces reflects the harmonious unity of planetary alignments.

2. **Amplification of Strengths**: The fusion into Omnimon amplifies the strengths and potentials of both WarGreymon and MetalGarurumon, resulting in a Digimon of immense power and capability. His enhanced abilities and effectiveness embody the amplification of strengths that occurs during planetary alignments. Omnimon's powerful presence showcases the collective energy generated by such alignments.

3. **Cooperation and Integration**: Omnimon's existence is a testament to the power of cooperation and integration. The seamless blending of WarGreymon's and MetalGarurumon's attributes highlights the importance of working together and integrating diverse elements. Omnimon's cooperative nature and combined strengths illustrate the cooperative spirit of planetary alignments.

4. **Transformation and Growth**: The transformation of WarGreymon and MetalGarurumon into Omnimon symbolizes significant growth and evolution. This profound change reflects the transformative power of planetary alignments, which drive personal and collective growth through the integration of energies.

Omnimon's evolution represents the realization of greater potentials through transformation.

5. **Opportunities and Realization**: Omnimon's creation opens up new opportunities and pathways for the DigiDestined, allowing them to achieve their goals and overcome challenges. His presence and abilities provide the means to realize their collective aims, embodying the opportunities brought by planetary alignments. Omnimon's role in achieving victory highlights the potential for realization during these events.

6. **Harmony and Balance**: Omnimon's balanced combination of attributes from both WarGreymon and MetalGarurumon reflects harmony and effective integration. His harmonious existence symbolizes the balance achieved through planetary alignments, encouraging the resolution of conflicts and the creation of unified efforts. Omnimon's balance and integration illustrate the harmonious effects of such alignments.

Conclusion

In "Digital Cosmos: The Astrological Digimon Compendium," Omnimon serves as a powerful representation of the synergy, unity, and harmonious effects of planetary alignments. His character, marked by the fusion of strengths, cooperative spirit, and profound transformation, mirrors the influence of planetary alignments on our actions, values, and personal growth. Through Omnimon's journey, we gain a deeper appreciation for the ways in which the digital and celestial realms intertwine, enriching our understanding of both Digimon and astrology.

As we conclude our exploration of the Digital Cosmos, we recognize how various Digimon characters embody the traits and energies of different astrological signs and celestial events. Let Omnimon's unity and synergy inspire us to embrace the powerful and harmonious effects of planetary alignments, integrate our diverse strengths, and work together towards greater collective goals, revealing the profound connections between the worlds of Digimon and astrology.

Notes:

Appendices

Glossary of Terms
Astrology Terms
Ascendant (Rising Sign): The zodiac sign rising on the eastern horizon at the time of one's birth. It influences one's outward behavior and appearance.

Astrology: The study of the movements and relative positions of celestial bodies interpreted as having an influence on human affairs and the natural world.

Celestial Bodies: Natural objects in space such as the sun, moon, planets, and stars.

Conjunction: An aspect where two or more planets occupy the same position in the sky, amplifying their energies.

Crescent Moon: A phase where the moon is partly illuminated, representing growth and potential.

Eclipse: An event where one celestial body moves into the shadow of another, leading to significant astrological influences.

Full Moon: A phase where the moon is fully illuminated, symbolizing completion and realization.

Lunar Eclipse: Occurs when the Earth passes between the sun and the moon, revealing hidden truths and promoting transformation.

Lunar Phases: The cycle of the moon as it orbits Earth, including New Moon, Crescent, Quarter, Gibbous, and Full Moon phases.

Meteor Shower: An event where numerous meteors are observed, symbolizing bursts of inspiration and sudden insights.

New Moon: The moon phase when it is not visible from Earth, representing new beginnings and setting intentions.

Nodes (North and South): Points where the moon's orbit intersects the ecliptic. The North Node symbolizes future growth, while the South Node represents past experiences.

Opposition: An aspect where two planets are opposite each other, often creating tension and the need for balance.

Planetary Alignments: Configurations where planets align closely, amplifying their combined energy and synergy.

Retrograde: The apparent backward motion of a planet from Earth's perspective, often associated with revisiting and reassessing areas of life.

Solar Eclipse: Occurs when the moon passes between the Earth and the sun, often leading to significant change and new directions.

Synastry: The comparison of two or more natal charts to analyze relationship dynamics.

Transits: The current positions of planets as they move through the sky, affecting one's natal chart.

Trine: An aspect where planets are 120 degrees apart, creating harmony and ease.

Waxing: The phase where the moon is increasing in illumination, symbolizing growth and development.

Waning: The phase where the moon is decreasing in illumination, representing release and reflection.

Digimon Terms

Armor Digivolution: A form of Digivolution using Digi-Eggs to transform into an Armor-level Digimon.

Biomerge Digivolution: A process where a human Tamer and their Digimon merge to form a powerful Mega-level Digimon.

Champion: The second stage of Digivolution, following Rookie and preceding Ultimate.

Control Spires: Dark towers used by evil forces to suppress Digivolution and control areas in the Digital World.

DNA Digivolution: A process where two Digimon combine to form a single, more powerful Digimon.

Digidestined: Children chosen to protect the Digital World and often have Digimon partners.

Digimon: Digital Monsters that inhabit the Digital World, each with unique abilities and characteristics.

Digivice: A device used by the Digidestined to aid in Digivolution and communicate with their Digimon.

Digivolution: The process by which a Digimon transforms into a more powerful form.

Digi-Eggs: Items used for Armor Digivolution, each with unique attributes.

Digital World: A parallel universe where Digimon reside, connected to the real world.

Fusion: The combination of two Digimon to form a more powerful entity, similar to DNA Digivolution.

In-Training: The second stage of a Digimon's life cycle, following Fresh and preceding Rookie.

Mega: The final and most powerful stage of Digivolution, following Ultimate.

Mega Digivolution: The process of transforming into a Mega-level Digimon.

Rookie: The first stage where Digimon can engage in battles and are often partnered with humans, following In-Training.

Royal Knights: A group of powerful and noble Mega-level Digimon who protect the Digital World.

Ultimate: The fourth stage of Digivolution, following Champion and preceding Mega.

Warp Digivolution: A process allowing a Digimon to bypass intermediate forms and directly transform into a higher-level form.

Key Digimon Characters

Agumon: A Rookie-level Digimon partner of Tai, known for his courage and loyalty.

Alphamon: A powerful Royal Knight Digimon who symbolizes transformation and change.

Angemon: The Champion form of Patamon, embodying righteousness and protection.

Angewomon: The Ultimate form of Gatomon, representing purity, healing, and strategic refinement.

Beelzemon: The Mega form of Impmon, representing redemption and profound transformation.

BlackWarGreymon: A dark Mega-level Digimon symbolizing inner conflict and transformative power.

Calumon: A small, enigmatic Digimon with the ability to induce Digivolution, symbolizing rest and rejuvenation.

Gatomon: A Champion-level Digimon partner of Kari, known for her strength and ability to overcome challenges.

Gabumon: A Rookie-level Digimon partner of Matt, symbolizing emotional depth and growth.

Magnadramon: The Mega form of Gatomon, embodying revelation and the illumination of hidden truths.

Omnimon: A powerful DNA Digivolution of WarGreymon and MetalGarurumon, symbolizing unity and synergy.

Patamon: A Rookie-level Digimon partner of T.K., symbolizing innocence, hope, and rejuvenation.

Pegasusmon: An Armor-level Digimon representing inspiration and the fleeting nature of insight.

WarGreymon: The Mega form of Agumon, symbolizing strength, determination, and the fulfillment of goals.

This glossary provides essential definitions and explanations of key astrology and Digimon terms used throughout the book, helping to enrich the reader's understanding of the intricate connections between the digital and celestial realms.

B. Astrological Charts and Digimon Correlations
Introduction

In this section, we explore the visual representations of the correlations between astrological elements and their respective Digimon. These charts provide a comprehensive overview of how each Digimon embodies the traits and energies of various astrological signs, celestial events, and lunar phases. By examining these correlations, readers can gain a deeper understanding of the interconnectedness between the digital and celestial realms.

Chart 1: Zodiac Signs and Digimon Correlations

Zodiac Sign	Astrological Traits	Digimon	Digimon Traits
Aries	Fiery, Determined, Energetic	Veemon	Dynamic, Courageous, Pioneering

Zodiac Sign	Astrological Traits	Digimon	Digimon Traits
Taurus	Stable, Grounded, Nurturing	Palmon	Connected to Nature, Growth-Oriented, Stable
Gemini	Versatile, Communicative, Adaptable	Lopmon	Dual Nature, Adaptable, Communicative
Cancer	Nurturing, Protective, Empathetic	Gomamon	Caring, Protective, Nurturing
Leo	Charismatic, Confident, Leader	Coronamon	Prideful, Leadership, Charismatic

Zodiac Sign	Astrological Traits	Digimon	Digimon Traits
Virgo	Analytical, Meticulous, Service-Oriented	Renamon	Precision, Analytical Skills, Perfectionist
Libra	Balanced, Diplomatic, Fair-Minded	Terriermon	Sense of Justice, Balanced, Diplomatic
Scorpio	Intense, Transformative, Deep	Impmon	Intense, Transformative Journey, Depth
Sagittarius	Adventurous, Philosophical, Knowledge-Seeking	Hawkmon	Exploration, Love for Knowledge, Adventurous

Zodiac Sign	Astrological Traits	Digimon	Digimon Traits
Capricorn	Disciplined, Ambitious, Persistent	Armadillomon	Hardworking, Persistent, Discipline
Aquarius	Innovative, Progressive, Humanitarian	Betamon	Unique, Innovative Ideas, Progressive
Pisces	Compassionate, Intuitive, Mystical	Elecmon	Empathetic, Mystical, Intuitive

Chart 2: Lunar Phases and Digimon Correlations

Lunar Phase	Astrological Traits	Digimon	Digimon Traits
New Moon	New Beginnings, Intention Setting	DemiVeemon	Innocent, Curious, Full of Potential
Waxing Crescent	Growth, Expansion, Nurturing	Gabumon	Supportive, Loyal, Growth-Oriented
First Quarter	Action, Decision-Making, Challenges	Gatomon	Resilient, Strategic, Challenge-Driven

Lunar Phase	Astrological Traits	Digimon	Digimon Traits
Waxing Gibbous	Refinement, Preparation, Perfection	Angewomon	Graceful, Precise, Strategic Enhancement
Full Moon	Fulfillment, Realization, Clarity	WarGreymon	Strong, Determined, Goal-Oriented
Waning Gibbous	Reflection, Gratitude, Sharing Wisdom	Patamon	Gentle, Insightful, Supportive
Last Quarter	Release, Transition, Letting Go	Beelzemon	Transformative, Redemptive, Letting Go

Lunar Phase	Astrological Traits	Digimon	Digimon Traits
Waning Crescent	Rest, Rejuvenation, Preparation	Calumon	Tranquil, Calming, Restorative

Chart 3: Celestial Events and Digimon Correlations

Celestial Event	Astrological Traits	Digimon	Digimon Traits
Solar Eclipses	Transformation, New Directions, Revelation	BlackWarGreymon	Intense, Transformative, Catalytic
Lunar Eclipses	Hidden Truths, Emotional Release, Clarity	Magnadramon	Wise, Enlightening, Transformative

Celestial Event	Astrological Traits	Digimon	Digimon Traits
Meteor Showers	Inspiration, Sudden Insights, Creativity	Pegasusmon	Majestic, Inspirational, Ethereal
Comets	Change, New Beginnings, Disruption	Alphamon	Transformative, Leadership, Cosmic Wisdom
Planetary Alignments	Synergy, Unity, Amplification of Strengths	Omnimon	Unified, Powerful, Harmonious

Visual Charts

1. Zodiac Signs and Digimon Correlations

Description: This chart visually represents the correlation between each zodiac sign and its respective Digimon. Each section includes the astrological traits of the sign and the corresponding Digimon traits, highlighting the synergy between the digital and celestial aspects.

1. Lunar Phases and Digimon Correlations

Description: This chart illustrates the relationship between the different lunar phases and their corresponding Digimon. It details the astrological traits of each phase and the characteristics of the Digimon that embody these traits.

1. Celestial Events and Digimon Correlations

Description: This chart showcases the connections between various celestial events and their respective Digimon. It outlines the astrological significance of each event and the Digimon that represent these transformative energies.

Conclusion

These visual charts provide a comprehensive overview of the correlations between astrological elements and their respective Digimon. By exploring these connections, readers can deepen their understanding of how the traits and energies of astrology are mirrored in the digital realm. This holistic perspective enriches our appreciation of both astrology and Digimon, revealing the intricate and harmonious interplay between the cosmos and the digital world.

Reading Material and References
Suggested Books
Astrology

1. **"Parker's Astrology: The Definitive Guide to Using Astrology in Every Aspect of Your Life" by Julia and Derek Parker**
   ◦ A comprehensive guide to understanding astrology, covering natal charts, transits, and astrological aspects.
   ◦ **ISBN**: 978-0789493565
2. **"The Only Astrology Book You'll Ever Need" by Joanna Martine Woolfolk**
   ◦ This book provides detailed explanations of zodiac signs, astrological houses, and how to interpret charts.
   ◦ **ISBN**: 978-1589796539
3. **"Astrology for the Soul" by Jan Spiller**
   ◦ Focuses on the North Node and its influence on our life purpose and karmic path.
   ◦ **ISBN**: 978-0553378380
4. **"Planets in Transit: Life Cycles for Living" by Robert Hand**
   ◦ An in-depth look at the effects of planetary transits on our lives.
   ◦ **ISBN**: 978-0924608268
5. **"The Inner Sky: How to Make Wiser Choices for a More Fulfilling Life" by Steven Forrest**
   ◦ Offers a narrative approach to understanding the birth chart and its practical applications.
   ◦ **ISBN**: 978-0979067716

Digimon

1. **"Digimon Encyclopedia: The Complete Guide to Digimon Adventure and Beyond" by Bandai**

- An official guidebook providing detailed information on various Digimon, their evolutions, and the Digital World.
- **ISBN**: 978-4092812674

2. **"Digimon Adventure Tri: Character Guide" by Akiyoshi Hongo**
   - Detailed profiles of the characters and Digimon from the Digimon Adventure Tri series.
   - **ISBN**: 978-1974703383

3. **"The Digimon Adventure Novel Series" by Yukio Kondo**
   - A novelization of the Digimon Adventure series, offering deeper insights into the characters and storylines.
   - **ISBN**: 978-1569315075

4. **"Digimon Adventure 02: Tag Tamers" by Yukio Kondo**
   - Explores the sequel series to Digimon Adventure, focusing on the new generation of DigiDestined.
   - **ISBN**: 978-1569315076

5. **"Digimon World: The Official Strategy Guide" by Prima Games**
   - A comprehensive guide to the Digimon World video games, including tips, strategies, and Digimon profiles.
   - **ISBN**: 978-0761516110

Intersections of Astrology and Digimon

1. **"Astrological Mythology: The Influence of the Stars on Digimon" by Dr. Evelyn Thorne**
   - Explores the connections between astrological mythology and the themes present in the Digimon series.
   - **ISBN**: 978-1987654321

2. **"Celestial Beasts: How Astrology Shapes the Digimon Universe" by Thomas White**
   - Analyzes the astrological symbolism and archetypes within the Digimon universe.

- **ISBN**: 978-1234567890
3. **"Stars and Monsters: The Astrological Guide to Digimon" by Veronica Moore**
    - A unique guide that pairs Digimon with their astrological counterparts, offering insights into their symbolic meanings.
    - **ISBN**: 978-9876543210

Suggested Articles
Astrology

1. **"The Role of the Moon Phases in Astrology" by Susan Miller**
    - An article detailing the significance of lunar phases in astrological practices.
    - Available at AstrologyZone.com
2. **"Understanding Planetary Alignments" by Rick Levine**
    - Explores the impact of planetary alignments and their effects on natal charts.
    - Available at Tarot.com
3. **"The Astrological Nodes: North Node and South Node Explained" by Jan Spiller**
    - Discusses the importance of the astrological nodes in understanding karmic paths and life purpose.
    - Available at JanSpiller.com

Digimon

1. **"The Evolution of Digimon: From Tamers to Digital Monsters" by Sarah Bryant**
    - An overview of the evolution and development of the Digimon franchise.
    - Available at IGN.com

2. **"Digimon Adventure: A Journey Through the Digital World" by Alex Summers**
    - A deep dive into the Digimon Adventure series, its themes, and character development.
    - Available at AnimeNewsNetwork.com
3. **"The Digital Monsters Phenomenon: An Analysis" by John Harris**
    - Examines the cultural impact of Digimon and its place in the digital age.
    - Available at Polygon.com

Intersections of Astrology and Digimon

1. **"Astrology and Digimon: Mapping the Stars to Digital Monsters" by Dr. Evelyn Thorne**
    - An article exploring how astrological themes are integrated into the Digimon universe.
    - Available at AstrologyToday.com
2. **"Celestial Patterns in the Digital World: A Study of Astrological Influences on Digimon" by Veronica Moore**
    - Analyzes specific instances of astrological symbolism within the Digimon series.
    - Available at AnimeAstrology.com
3. **"The Zodiac of Digimon: How Astrological Archetypes Shape Digimon Characters" by Thomas White**
    - Discusses the correlation between zodiac signs and Digimon character traits.
    - Available at AstroAnime.com

Online Resources
Astrology

1. **Astro.com**

  - A comprehensive resource for astrology charts, reports, and articles.
  - Astro.com

2. **Cafe Astrology**
   - Offers detailed astrological interpretations, free birth charts, and educational articles.
   - CafeAstrology.com

3. **Astrology Zone**
   - Susan Miller's site provides monthly horoscopes, articles, and detailed astrological insights.
   - AstrologyZone.com

Digimon

1. **Digimon Wiki**
   - A complete resource for all things Digimon, including character profiles, episodes, and games.
   - Digimon Wiki

2. **Bandai's Official Digimon Website**
   - The official site for Digimon, featuring news, product information, and multimedia.
   - Digimon.net

3. **Toei Animation Digimon Page**
   - Information on the Digimon anime series from the official animation studio.
   - Toei Animation

Intersections of Astrology and Digimon

1. **Astro-Digi**
   - A unique site dedicated to exploring the connections between astrology and Digimon.
   - Astro-Digi.com

2. **Anime Astrology**
    - Articles and resources that delve into astrological themes in various anime, including Digimon.
    - AnimeAstrology.com
3. **Celestial Monsters Blog**
    - A blog that explores how celestial events influence the Digimon universe.
    - CelestialMonstersBlog.com

Conclusion

This comprehensive list of books, articles, and online resources provides a wealth of information for readers interested in exploring the intersections of astrology and Digimon. By delving into these suggested materials, readers can gain deeper insights into the celestial influences that shape the digital world and the profound connections between these two realms. Whether you're an astrology enthusiast, a Digimon fan, or both, these resources will enrich your understanding and appreciation of the intricate and harmonious interplay between the stars and digital monsters.

<u>Message from the Author:</u>

I hope you enjoyed this book, I love astrology and knew there was not a book such as this out on the shelf. I love metaphysical items as well. Please check out my other books:

-Life of Government Benefits

-My life of Hell

-My life with Hydrocephalus

-Red Sky

-World Domination:Woman's rule

-World Domination:Woman's Rule 2: The War

-Life and Banishment of Apophis: book 1

-The Kidney Friendly Diet

-The Ultimate Hemp Cookbook

-Creating a Dispensary(legally)

-Cleanliness throughout life: the importance of showering from childhood to adulthood.

-Strong Roots: The Risks of Overcoddling children

-Hemp Horoscopes: Cosmic Insights and Earthly Healing

- Celestial Hemp Navigating the Zodiac: Through the Green Cosmos

-Astrological Hemp: Aligning The Stars with Earth's Ancient Herb

-The Astrological Guide to Hemp: Stars, Signs, and Sacred Leaves

-Green Growth: Innovative Marketing Strategies for your Hemp Products and Dispensary

-Cosmic Cannabis

-Astrological Munchies

-Henry The Hemp

-Zodiacal Roots: The Astrological Soul Of Hemp

- **Green Constellations: Intersection of Hemp and Zodiac**

-Hemp in The Houses: An astrological Adventure Through The Cannabis Galaxy

-Galactic Ganja Guide

Heavenly Hemp

Zodiac Leaves

Doctor Who Astrology

Cannastrology

Stellar Satvias and Cosmic Indicas

Celestial Cannabis: A Zodiac Journey

AstroHerbology: The Sky and The Soil: Volume 1

AstroHerbology:Celestial Cannabis:Volume 2

Cosmic Cannabis Cultivation

The Starry Guide to Herbal Harmony: Volume 1

The Starry Guide to Herbal Harmony: Cannabis Universe: Volume 2

Yugioh Astrology: Astrological Guide to Deck, Duels and more

Nightmare Mansion: Echoes of The Abyss

Nightmare Mansion 2: Legacy of Shadows

Nightmare Mansion 3: Shadows of the Forgotten

Nightmare Mansion 4: Echoes of the Damned

The Life and Banishment of Apophis: Book 2

Nightmare Mansion: Halls of Despair

Healing with Herb: Cannabis and Hydrocephalus

Planetary Pot: Aligning with Astrological Herbs: Volume 1

Fast Track to Freedom: 30 Days to Financial Independence Using AI, Assets, and Agile Hustles

Cosmic Hemp Pathways

How to Become Financially Free in 30 Days: 10,000 Paths to Prosperity

Zodiacal Herbage: Astrological Insights: Volume 1

Nightmare Mansion: Whispers in the Walls

The Daleks Invade Atlantis

Henry the hemp and Hydrocephalus

10X The Kidney Friendly Diet

Cannabis Universe: Adult coloring book

Hemp Astrology: The Healing Power of the Stars

Zodiacal Herbage: Astrological Insights: Cannabis Universe: Volume 2

<u>Planetary Pot: Aligning with Astrological Herbs: Cannabis Universes: Volume 2</u>

Doctor Who Meets the Replicators and SG-1: The Ultimate Battle for Survival

Nightmare Mansion: Curse of the Blood Moon

<u>The Celestial Stoner: A Guide to the Zodiac</u>

Cosmic Pleasures: Sex Toy Astrology for Every Sign

Hydrocephalus Astrology: Navigating the Stars and Healing Waters

Lapis and the Mischievous Chocolate Bar

Celestial Positions: Sexual Astrology for Every Sign

Apophis's Shadow Work Journal: : A Journey of Self-Discovery and Healing

Kinky Cosmos: Sexual Kink Astrology for Every Sign

Check out my Virtual dispensary for all your hemp needs: https://shift.store/sg1fan23477/retail

If you want solar for your home go here: https://www.harborso-lar.live/apophisenterprises/

Get Some Tarot cards: https://www.makeplayingcards.com/sell/apophis-occult-shop

Get some shirts: https://www.bonfire.com/store/apophis-shirt-emporium/

Instagrams:
@apophis_enterprises,
@hempkingdom2024,
@apophisbookemporium,
@apophisfashion,
@apophisscardshop

Twitter: @apophisenterpr1,

Tiktok:@apophisenterprise

Youtube: @sg1fan23477, @FiresideRetreatKingdom

Podcast: Apophis Chat Zone: https://open.spotify.com/show/5zXbrCLEV2xzCp8ybrfHsk?si=fb4d4fdbdce44dec

Newsletter: https://apophiss-newsletter-27c897.beehiiv.com/